The God We Do Not Know

The God We Do Not Know

Jim Thomson

FOREWORD BY
Gary Major

RESOURCE *Publications* • Eugene, Oregon

THE GOD WE DO NOT KNOW

Copyright © 2016 Jim Thomson. All rights reserved. Except for brief quotations in critical publications or reviews, no part of this book may be reproduced in any manner without prior written permission from the publisher. Write: Permissions, Wipf and Stock Publishers, 199 W. 8th Ave., Suite 3, Eugene, OR 97401.

Resource Publications
An Imprint of Wipf and Stock Publishers
199 W. 8th Ave., Suite 3
Eugene, OR 97401

www.wipfandstock.com

PAPERBACK ISBN: 978-1-4982-9855-1
HARDCOVER ISBN: 978-1-4982-5588-2
EBOOK ISBN: 978-1-4982-9856-8

Manufactured in the U.S.A.

Unless otherwise indicated, all Scripture quotations are from The Holy Bible, English Standard Version®. Copyright © 2001 by Crossway Bibles, a division of Good News Publishers. Used by permission. All rights reserved.

Scripture quotations marked (CEV) are from the Contemporary English Version Copyright © 1991, 1992, 1995 by American Bible Society. Used by Permission.

Scripture quotations designated NKJV are from The Holy Bible, New King James Version®. Copyright © 1979, 1980, 1982 by Thomas Nelson, Inc. Used by permission. All rights reserved.

Scripture quotations taken from The Holy Bible, New International Version® NIV®. Copyright © 1973, 1978, 1984, 2011 by Biblica, Inc.™ Used by permission. All rights reserved worldwide.

Contents

Foreword by Gary Major | vii
Introduction | ix

1. The God of Insignificance | 1
2. The God of Discomfort | 12
3. The God of Dust and Glory | 31
4. The God Who Is Perfect | 39
5. The God Who Is Like a Child | 52
6. The Unexpected God | 61
7. The God Who Is Gentle and Lowly in Heart | 72
8. The God of Equality | 84
9. The God of Fear | 101
10. The God of Love | 110

Bibliography | 127

Foreword

OVER THE MANY YEARS that I have known Jim, we have spent many enjoyable mornings drinking coffee while discussing the incomprehensible nature of God. As I read through the preliminary drafts for this book, *The God We Do Not Know*, it was as if I was having a conversation with him as he wrote it. The truths we discussed in those times together were often stunning. The Lord truly is so much bigger, so much more detailed, and so much more wonderful, awesome, fearful, and amazing than we could ever imagine. The exceptionally daunting truth is that He wants to know us, and yet, in our finite beings, we can only know Him in a fraction of the way that He can know us.

Getting to know God better is a fundamental call to any Christian, but it can be distinctly uncomfortable. When we come to the realization that the Lord is not who we think He is or want Him to be, it forces us to change our outlook and our world view. We don't often, if ever, think of God as a God of insignificance or the God of dust and glory. Or what it means that He is the God who is perfect.

This book challenges us, the readers, to gain a new perspective on the God we do not know. Like Jim, I welcome you to the journey.

Gary Major
Technical Project Manager

Introduction

How does one write about a God who is so glorious and immense that He overwhelms our ability to describe Him?
With an admission of humbling inadequacy.
But humility is a funny thing. Once one lays claim to it, it vanishes.
Well, written with great love, then. However, my love for God is infirm, like a mist that shrinks away when touched by the heat of the sun.
No, this author has no delusions about his inability to engage in the task at hand. We are attempting to gain insight into a God who demolishes us, it seems, at every turn. He possesses mind-bending intelligence, creativity, power, and love. Therefore, if we truly want to know Him, His truths will inevitably lead us into rough, unpredictable—but wondrous—terrain. We must investigate these truths; be stormed, shattered, and swept away, in love, by them.
The Lord our God compels us to know Him; in fact, He demands it. He demands it because knowing Him is for our good.
He demands it because He loves us.
I do not claim to possess anything that approximates a satisfactory knowledge of the God with whom I have fallen more deeply in love, by His grace, in the over forty years I have walked with Him. Nor is there any assertion within these pages to an attainment of exclusive or complete knowledge of God. That would be the pinnacle of foolishness. Future additions and updates will

Introduction

surely be necessary. Nevertheless, imprudent as it may seem, this book has been written because the biblical truths contained herein have challenged me to the core of who I am and have caused me to walk in even greater awe of our great, loving, unfathomable God.

I invite you to join me on this pilgrimage with our Father and our Savior, Jesus.

Welcome to the journey.

1

The God of Insignificance

*God chose what is low and despised in the world,
even things that are not, to bring to nothing things that are,
so that no human being might boast in the presence of God.*[1]

~ Paul to the church at Corinth

SINGERS AND SUPERSTARS, ACTORS and artists, sometimes opine about the blessings and blights of fame. Although celebrities realize notoriety is accompanied, understandably, by intrusive aggravations, few would be willing to renounce their renown because of it. Most of us, like them, consider the prospect of a life of insignificance as a condition to be most dreaded. The pressure from our cultures to "be somebody" is strong. Some have even predicted that one day, at least for a few minutes, the bright spotlight of popularity will shine on everyone in the world. Such pundits probably would not be surprised by our contemporary vanity-driven attempts to gain those brief moments of recognition. However, as reality irrupts, that search for significance turns out to be obstinately elusive, although it may require the entire sweep of one's life to come to terms with that unsettling truth. Very few of us will be considered "somebodies" by the world's measure. Thus, we

1. 1 Corinthians 1:28–29.

may attempt to rid ourselves of the consequences of that certainty by any means necessary, and many of those efforts—perhaps all of them—are darkly destructive. Happily, it may be surprising to discover that being somebody—noteworthy and important in the world's eyes—is in fundamental opposition to the Christian God's truth about one's significance.

For many of us, the sense of feeling insignificant or "less than" began early in our lives. Perhaps when the neighborhood kids gathered to play a game, you were picked last. You may have struggled in school, and it seemed obvious that other students were brighter than you. A chorus of voices, perhaps including those of your own parents, may have attempted to impress upon you the inevitability of a life of inferiority. Maybe you were not as pretty or handsome as other children and didn't meet the standards of desirability in your culture. Hearing a person more athletic, attractive, or intelligent shout, "Loser!" in your direction was an announcement to everyone within earshot that you were on the pathetic, losing side of the way things were.

If this is you, take heart. This is precisely the kind of person whom the Lord chooses.

The Lord's Preference: Those Who Are Insignificant

Through whom does the Lord God, the Creator of all things, choose to glorify Himself? Paul gave us the answer to that question in 1 Corinthians 1:26–29: God chooses people who are foolish, weak, low, despised, and are nothing by the world's measure. The following are definitions for these words from the Greek.

The first word "foolish," is straightforward. It simply means "foolish or stupid."[2]

"Weak" is defined as "of relative ineffectiveness, whether external or inward."[3]

---

2. Bauer, *Greek-English Lexicon*, 663 s.v. (under the word) μωρός.
3. Ibid., 143 s.v. ἀσθενής 2, b.

"Low" is "insignificant."[4]

Something that is "despised" is "an entity (that) has no merit or worth."[5]

"Things that are not" is uncomfortably frank. God chooses people who, in the eyes of the world, do not even exist.[6]

Why does the Lord choose such people? Paul told us:

- to shame the wise,
- to shame the strong,
- to bring to nothing things that are.

The final result of that shaming and bringing to nothingness is "so that no human being might boast in the presence of God."

The significance that much of the world struggles to obtain is, astonishingly, an aspiration that places us in opposition to our Creator. He calls us to conform to His example of humility, not to that of a fallen race, those who in our eyes are substantial but, as James says, possesses no more substance than the morning fog: "What is your life? For you are a mist that appears for a little time and then vanishes."[7]

We are like grass that withers in the heat of the sun; spring flowers that fade and fall as they grow old.

The Least of All People

The truth about those whom God chooses is found not only in Paul's first letter to the Corinthians. According to all of Scripture, it is evident that the powerful Lord God of the universe chooses people who are, to sum up, worthless in the world's way of thinking. The Word of God plainly says this, although we shrink back from this biblical reality. Let's start our study at the beginnings of Israel, chronicled in Genesis. Who was Abraham, for example? Before

---

4. Ibid., 9 s.v. ἀγενής.
5. Ibid., 352 s.v. ἐξουθενέω 1.
6. Ibid., 283 s.v. εἰμί 1.
7. James 4:14b.

the Lord called him, he was simply a man whom his father had taken to a place called Haran, a city in Mesopotamia, which was a center for the cult of the moon god, Sin. Had Abram achieved any significance when the Lord called him? No, he was just a man living in a pagan city. Why did God pick him over any other man in Haran? We do not know. Actually, we do, because Paul tells us: Abram was insignificant, foolish, and weak. He is the prototype for those whom the Lord chooses.

Leah was a woman who was unloved by her husband, Jacob. He rejected her from the beginning. When Jacob had been fooled by his uncle and had marital relations with Leah instead of Rachel, Jacob still could not bring himself to love her. However, this verse will give us an insight into how God thinks: "When the LORD saw that Leah was hated, he opened her womb, but Rachel was barren."[8] The Lord favored the woman who was despised, and she bore six sons, one of whom was Judah, the forefather of Jesus.

Who was Joseph when the Lord gave him a dream that changed his life and the lives of everyone in his family; indeed, that so dramatically changed the history of Israel? The second-to-youngest son in a family whose siblings detested him so greatly that they wanted to kill him but instead wholesaled him as a slave to a caravan of traders en route to Egypt.

Who was Moses when the Lord called by means of a voice in a burning bush? An inessential shepherd in the wilderness—and an impetuous murderer who had fled from Pharaoh.

Who was Gideon before the angel came and sat under the terebinth tree at Ophrah while that mighty man of valor threshed wheat in the winepress? We are not told. He was just a man who was a member of the weakest clan in Manasseh and the least in his father's house,[9] laboring in secret to ensure his family's survival.

What about the other judges, deliverers, kings, and prophets of Israel? What was it that caused the Lord to choose them?

Deborah was a woman and a prophetess, a member of a culturally unimpressive gender class.

---

8. Genesis 29:31.
9. Judges 6:15.

The God of Insignificance

Jephthah was the son of a prostitute.

At first glance, Samson seems to be an exception. He was a supernaturally strong man. However, his strength came from that which is not strong at all—his hair, which was a symbol of a Nazarite, one who is set apart before God. When Samson rejected that unique, godly place, he became a man who thought his strength was his own and therefore regressed into someone through whom God could not be glorified. It wasn't until he was blind, bound, debilitated, and determined to die that he became weak enough for Israel's enemies to be substantially destroyed, so the Lord was glorified, not Samson.

Who was Ruth? A woman from among the Moabites, a pagan people who worshiped the god Chemosh; a widow living on the edge of starvation. She became the wife of Boaz, the father of Jesse, the father of David, the forefather of Jesus.

Who was the only person who was faithful and thus spared, along with her family, the devastating destruction wrought upon Jericho? Rahab, a prostitute, who ended up being in the lineage of Jesus.

Who was David when the Lord chose him as king? The youngest son in the family, a child so inconsequential, so forgotten, that Jesse did not even bother to call him to the house when the prophet Samuel visited and summoned all the sons to be gathered. David fits well into the description of those whom God chooses. He was almost non-existent in the eyes of his father.

Who was Esther, who helped deliver God's people from annihilation? She was an orphaned female who was picked to become a concubine in the harem of the king of Persia.

Who was Elijah? A Tishbite, a man from an irrelevant village called Tishbe, a place unknown to world history.

Who was Elisha? A farmer.

Who was Daniel? Although he was apparently of royal descent, he was also a captive, a displaced person, a citizen of a conquered nation, residing in a foreign culture.

Who was Jeremiah when the Lord called him to prophesy to Judah? A priest from Anathoth, a city about which almost nothing is known.

Who was Isaiah when the Lord called him to prophesy to Israel? He was the son of Amoz and a nephew of Amaziah, a murdered king of Judah with a tainted record of rulership.

Who was Hosea when the Lord called him to prophesy to Judah? Again, information is sparse. He is introduced as Hosea, son of Beeri.

Who was Amos? He tells us in his response to Amaziah the priest: "I was no prophet, nor a prophet's son, but I was a herdsman and a dresser of sycamore figs."[10]

Who was Malachi? We do not know.

The prophet Zechariah? Berechiah's son and the grandson of Iddo.

The prophet Joel? He was Pethuel's son.

Do we need to continue?

Orphans. Widows. Farmers. Forgotten children. Disregarded, poor, and powerless women. People chosen by God because they were unimpressive from birth or diminished in some way so God could be glorified, not them.

Insignificance in the New Testament

The Lord's use of insignificance continued in the New Testament. The most outstanding example is the Lord Jesus, the Creator of all things, who came to earth as a completely helpless baby, born to a poor couple in an obscure place called Bethlehem, a small town in a little-known, weak nation that had been conquered yet once again by a very powerful one. Why would the Lord God incarnate be born, grow up, minister, die, rise from the dead, and ascend into the heavens in an undistinguished part of the world the Romans called Judea? Why was it His plan that no one outside of the immediate area would even be aware of His existence while He walked

---

10. Amos 7:14.

The God of Insignificance

the earth? When we read about the individuals the Lord chose in the Old Testament, they are types of the One who would become the least of all.

We could also ask, who were the disciples of Jesus when He called them to follow? In our way of thinking, it would seem unwise to choose only twelve very fallible men to establish His Church. What notoriety, status, or importance did any of these individuals possess when they were chosen? Peter, Andrew, James, and John were fishermen; Matthew, a despised tax collector.

Who was the only person in the Bible about whom Jesus said this? "Truly, I say to you, wherever this gospel is proclaimed in the whole world, what she has done will also be told in memory of her."[11] A woman, probably a prostitute, who anointed Jesus for His burial. We do not even know her name.

Who were some of the first people to whom Jesus revealed Himself after His resurrection? Mary Magdalene, Joanna, and Mary, the mother of James, women whose sworn statements in that culture were almost worthless. Jesus' disciples did not even believe them after they returned and explained what they had seen at the tomb.[12] Why would the Lord choose such inferior individuals to be the first to testify about the greatest event in the history of the world?

Paul became an apostle of Jesus Christ only after he lost all of his self-righteous Pharisaical authority and status. Yet, he joyously proclaimed, "But whatever gain I had, I counted as loss for the sake of Christ. Indeed, I count everything as loss because of the surpassing worth of knowing Christ Jesus my Lord. For his sake I have suffered the loss of all things and count them as rubbish, in order that I may gain Christ."[13]

The picture that is illustrated for us in Scripture should be clear, and it is probable that Paul was thinking of the individuals in Scripture and drawing from his own knowledge and experience when he penned those Holy-Spirit-inspired words to the

---

11. Matthew 26:6–13; Luke 7:36–50; Mark 14:3–9.
12. Luke 24:10–11.
13. Philippians 3:7–8.

Corinthians. Regardless of how we define significance in our cultures, it is biblically evident that the Lord chooses inconsequential individuals living in inauspicious places through whom to accomplish His hard-to-comprehend purposes.

He is the God of insignificance.

However, this should not amaze us. He is the God we do not know.

Has the Lord Been Thinking Clearly?

Is it surprising that God chooses people who are foolish, weak, and despised? Does the Lord know what He's doing? Absurd question, clearly, but it needs to be asked in light of the staggering dissonance between His ways and ours. The answer to the question is, of course, yes, because in comparison to what He accomplishes by His incomparable power, everything we do is foolish and weak. He told the disciples plainly that without Him they could do nothing at all.[14] Our amazing God is not necessarily looking for culturally impressive people in order to accomplish His irrational and powerful will. He is not put to shame at all if we are humiliated or derided. After all, Jesus was. He "had no form or majesty that we should look at him, and no beauty that we should desire him," and "was despised and rejected by men."[15] The prophets were disdained and dismissed. Noah, Moses, David, Micaiah, Elijah, Isaiah, Jeremiah, Micah, and Amos were all scorned either by their families, the world, or religious leaders. Jesus' disciples were viewed as "uneducated, common men."[16] Do we truly want to be included in that noble company? We prefer to be cool. Attractive. Culturally clued in and appealingly humorous. We have very little idea how to deal with these words of blessing: "Blessed are you when people hate you and when they exclude you and revile you and spurn your name as evil, on account of the Son of Man! Rejoice in that day,

---

14. John 15:5.
15. Isaiah 53:2b–3a.
16. Acts 4:13.

and leap for joy, for behold, your reward is great in heaven; for so their fathers did to the prophets."[17]

We want to be influential and well-liked, but apparently, it is not our preference to be blessed or have great reward in heaven.

Instead of displaying how strong and worthy of notice we are, we should strive to reveal how weak and unimportant we are. Instead of proclaiming our strengths, let us endeavor to boast of the things that show our weakness, as Paul did.[18] Instead of contending for significance, we should contend for *in*significance. This is the way our God, He who is lowly in heart, chooses to do business. When we read about those whom the Lord selected throughout Scripture, we cannot avoid this inescapable truth. We should line up on the side of the basketball court where all the wimps and losers stand.

In spite of a multitude of biblical examples, this truth seems just too difficult for me to grasp. Even though I see it in Scripture, all too often, as soon as He chooses me and performs something wonderful and God-glorifying through me, the shift from being "nothing" to desiring to be "something" remains just one, little, intoxicating step away.

The cultural pundits were right. Everybody wants to be somebody and experience their fleeting moments of fame.

According to Our Thinking, God's Plan Will Not Work

I know the confounding questions that troop through my head like disoriented soldiers when I consider the practical application of this truth. How in the world would God's blueprint for choosing the lowly and irrelevant ever work? How would we get anything done? The choices that God makes are so contrary to my thinking that I cannot even imagine their implementation. This, however, unnerves me. It frightens me because this is exactly the

---

17. Luke 6:22–23.
18. 2 Corinthians 11:30.

way the Jews thought at the time of Jesus. They simply could not, by any stretch of the imagination or their knowledge of Scripture, understand that their Messiah would be a despised and weakened sacrificial Lamb. Today, we look back at Scripture and ask, "How could they have missed it? How could they not have considered Isaiah 53? How could they not have put together Micah 5:2 and Isaiah 7:14?" I might also ask in the same way, "How could we have overlooked 1 Corinthians 1:25–29, concerning those whom God chooses? How could we have not understood the overwhelming testimony of Scripture in respect to those whom God selected to do His will? How could we have ignored the glaring truth that Jesus Himself, our example, was considered of little consequence and even despised in the eyes of the Jewish and Roman worlds, as were His disciples?"

Bringing to Nothing the Things That Are

In light of the truth from 1 Corinthians 1 and New and Old Testament examples, we should think that our claims about our influence and success—"things that are"—are not assertions that the Lord would especially care for. Perhaps that is far too generous. He does not want them in His presence at all, because His stated intent is "to bring to nothing things that are." This sovereign activity of God sounds a bit destructive. Or perhaps humiliating. Or both. He ordains this so no one might boast in His presence. He will not be deterred in His purpose. Therefore, should any person or entity that operates with a perception that he, she, or it is "something," be a bit alarmed in light of this truth? I certainly am. Being "something" is my default response, it seems, concerning how I want to be perceived.

So, fellow Christian brothers and sisters, welcome to the appalling, wonderful fellowship of the foolish and the frail—welcome to fellowship of Jesus. We are people who are never to boast about ourselves and our attainments. If our desire is to understand His will and please Him, we should deny any effort to portray ourselves as significant.

There Are No Undemanding Answers

What shall we do? There are no undemanding answers. I have come to realize that following Jesus may be simple, but it is not easy. Therefore, this is where any solutions would begin: with Him and His turning-our-religious-world-upside-down truth. All that we need to know about how to follow His astonishing ways are in Him and His Word. We should realize the life-upending importance of His uncomfortable realities and humbly bring our questions to Him. It is wise to ask Him how to walk in His truth, life, and way. He is everything there is, and all that can be offered. This is the right, good, and devoted place to abide in the light of the knowledge of the God we do not know.

2

The God of Discomfort

Share in suffering as a good soldier of Christ Jesus.[1]

~ Paul to Timothy

WHEN LAURIE AND I lived in India, our job assignment was to mentor national pastors and leaders. One evening, on our way to a Bible study with a small group of believers, I became violently ill and vomited repeatedly inside the church van. I became so weak in just a matter of minutes that I had to be lifted out of the vehicle like a ragdoll, put in a wheelchair, and admitted to a hospital. I had never experienced this level of sickness in my life.

On another night, not long after that incident, I awoke in our bed fully dressed. As I looked around, I saw that several of our friends were in the room. An ambulance had come to take me to the hospital—again. I had had a seizure in my sleep. I had never had a seizure before. Thankfully, my hospital stay was brief.

Shortly after we arrived in India, I began to suffer from severe allergies, and my nose ran like a faucet. That, in conjunction with the pollution of the large city in which we lived, caused me to get asthma. I had never had asthma before. However, this condition

---

1. 2 Timothy 2:3.

eventually necessitated our departure from India. Even with a rescue inhaler, I had difficulty breathing sometimes.

Could the Lord have prevented these illnesses and healed the allergies and the asthma so that we could have continued our ministry there? Yes, indeed. All things are possible for Him.[2] Nevertheless, He did not.

My trouble in India is trivial compared to the trials of very many believers. The reader may be familiar with significantly more upsetting, even tragic, accounts in his or her own life of diseases that were not cured, premature babies who did not survive, and accidents that could have been averted. These situations bring forth questions, cause doubt, and challenge faith. Therefore, a legitimate question can and should be asked: Is it possible that our loving God and Father would ever cause His people to suffer discomfort? The biblical answer to this question is not one we would prefer to hear. Both the Old and New Testaments are bursting with accounts of the discomfited saints of God.

God's People: A Fellowship of Discomfort

According to evidence throughout Scripture, it is clear that God, according to His gracious will and purpose, permitted or caused His people to experience difficulties. Here are a few notable examples:

After losing almost everything, including all of his children, Job was reduced to scraping his boils with a piece of broken pottery. Because of his suffering, he reasoned that God had become his enemy.[3]

The Lord asked Abraham to sacrifice Isaac, the very son He Himself had promised.[4]

---

2. Mark 14:36.
3. Job 2:7–8; 13:24.
4. Genesis 22:2.

Joseph, a slave in Potiphar's house in Egypt, was falsely accused of sexual assault by his master's wife and thrown into prison.[5]

God allowed His people to suffer in bondage as slaves in Egypt for hundreds of years. He even told Abraham generations earlier that this oppression would come to pass.[6] As powerful and God-glorifying as the accounts of the Exodus and defeat of Egypt and its gods are, if you had been born during the four hundred years of captivity, all that you would have known as one of God's people was slavery. Unless you were a member of Jacob's family who first came to Egypt or in the generation of the Exodus, you would have been born a slave, and you would have died a slave.

Even in that great deliverance, when the Lord struck Egypt with pestilence, God's people suffered the first three plagues along with the Egyptians when the Nile turned to blood and when the land was overwhelmed with frogs and gnats.[7]

After the Exodus from Egypt, Moses was opposed by his own people in the wilderness,[8] and they attempted to overthrow him.[9] In fact, his own brother Aaron and sister Miriam rose up against him because he had married a Cushite woman of whom they did not approve.[10]

David was persecuted and relentlessly pursued by King Saul, who wanted to murder him,[11] even though David was an especially close friend of Saul's son, Jonathan, and twice demonstrated that he had no desire to kill the anointed ruler.[12] After David became king, his own son, Absalom, dethroned and humiliated him.[13]

---

5. Genesis 39.
6. Genesis 15:13.
7. Exodus 7:14—8:23.
8. Exodus 17:1–3.
9. Numbers 16:1–3.
10. Numbers 12:1–2.
11. 1 Samuel 18:10–11.
12. 1 Samuel 24, 26.
13. 2 Samuel 15.

Absalom was subsequently killed by Joab, in defiance of David's instructions, which caused the king great grief.[14]

The Psalms abound with outcries for deliverance from the troubles experienced by David and the other psalmists. Here is but one example:

> For my soul is full of troubles,
> and my life draws near to Sheol.
> I am counted among those
> who go down to the pit;
> I am a man who has no strength,
> like one set loose among the dead,
> like the slain that lie in the grave,
> like those whom you remember no more,
> for they are cut off from your hand.
> (Psalm 88:3–5).

Solomon, with all his wisdom, wrote that man's "days are full of sorrow, and his work is a vexation. Even in the night his heart does not rest."[15]

After preaching repentance to Nineveh, Jonah sat under the shade of a plant to seek respite from the sweltering heat. The Lord sent a worm to sever the life of that small measure of comfort, even though Jonah was suffering so greatly that he wanted to die.[16]

Jeremiah was threatened with death and lowered into the muck at the bottom of a well for speaking the word of the Lord.[17]

Jesus told Peter that Satan demanded to sift him like wheat and that He would pray for him, but He gave no promise that He would stop Satan's activity against him.[18]

---

14. 2 Samuel 18:33.
15. Ecclesiastes 2:23.
16. Jonah 4:7–8.
17. Jeremiah 18:23, 38:1–6.
18. Luke 22:31–32.

James, one of the three apostles who were closest to Jesus, was beheaded, and Peter was imprisoned.[19]

Paul and Silas were beaten with rods because of their ministry and locked up in jail.[20] Paul was again incarcerated[21] and wrote in his letter to the Corinthians that he had also been whipped, stoned, shipwrecked and adrift at sea, hungry, thirsty, sleepless, and in danger from, well, just about everyone.[22] Tradition tells us he was eventually martyred.

Church tradition also tells us that all of Jesus' twelve disciples, except John (and Judas, of course), died as martyrs. John was imprisoned for a time on the Isle of Patmos.[23]

In the troubling passage that follows, the Lord tells His people what will happen after someone called "the beast" appears in Revelation 13:7–10. "Also it was allowed to make war on the saints and to conquer them. And authority was given it over every tribe and people and language and nation, and all who dwell on earth will worship it, everyone whose name has not been written before the foundation of the world in the book of life of the Lamb who was slain. If anyone has an ear, let him hear: If anyone is to be taken captive, to captivity he goes; if anyone is to be slain with the sword, with the sword must he be slain. Here is a call for the endurance and faith of the saints."

When the Lord warns Christians that they will be conquered and are in need of endurance and faith, it should cause them to sit up and take notice. Without dispute, this will be a life-threatening and grievous time for the followers of Jesus Christ. Until the end of the Church Age, God will allow His people to be exposed to arduous hardship.

---

19. Acts 12:1–5.
20. Acts 16:22–24.
21. 2 Timothy 2:8–9.
22. 2 Corinthians 11:21–33.
23. Revelation 1:9.

The God of Trouble and Comfort

Yet, in spite of the misery and grief experienced by God's people, the Lord is a God of comfort: "Blessed be the God and Father of our Lord Jesus Christ, the Father of mercies and God of all comfort, who comforts us in all our affliction, so that we may be able to comfort those who are in any affliction, with the comfort with which we ourselves are comforted by God."[24]

Jesus told us that the Lord will comfort those who are grieving: "Blessed are those who mourn, for they shall be comforted."[25]

Jesus also said, "In the world you will have tribulation. But take heart; I have overcome the world."[26]

Experiencing tribulation in the world is a promise from Jesus Himself. Thankfully, our experience with trouble and distress is not the end of the matter. Jesus finished His statement by gloriously proclaiming that He had overcome the world. He is our hope, comfort, and ultimate Victor. In addition, we have this elegant, faith-filled pronouncement from the apostle Paul: "For I consider that the sufferings of this present time are not worthy *to be compared* with the glory which shall be revealed in us."[27]

Everyone, including followers of Jesus Christ, will encounter suffering of one kind or another in their brief lives on this planet. However, Christians are encouraged to faithfully believe that all our hardships will pale in comparison to the eternal glory that is to come.

The Lord gives both comfort and discomfort? Victory along with tribulation and defeat? Yes. The reality is that the Lord's peace and comfort become truly meaningful only when peace and comfort are absent. As was noted, He "comforts us in all our *affliction.*"[28] Before peace and comfort arrive, conflict and discomfort break out—which may have been caused by God Himself.

---

24. 2 Corinthians 1:3–4.
25. Matthew 5:4.
26. John 16:33b.
27. Romans 8:18 NKJV.
28. 2 Corinthians 1:4a, italics added.

The God We Do Not Know

We Naturally Prefer Comfort

There are very few people on the planet, who, if given the option, would not choose to live a trouble-free and pleasant life. If it is available, we will use air conditioning or electric fans to make us more comfortable when we are sweltering in the heat. Without question, we prefer health over sickness. If possible, we would rather have money in our pockets or the bank versus a lack of funds, a life of poverty, and possible economic devastation. A new car that is less likely to break down on the road is better than an undependable junker held together with duct tape and baling wire. However, even an old car is preferable to long journeys on foot or stifling, crowded buses. We like our cupboards stocked with food rather than shelves that are empty. We would prefer not to be beaten and imprisoned for our faith. The downside to this reasonable need for comfort is our tendency to become at ease, and that predisposition may lead to a creeping, sleepy self-satisfaction. If we are not careful, this contentment can be deadly to our faith, because we are in danger of no longer being in desperate need of God.

There is a reason Jesus said, "Blessed are the poor in spirit, for theirs is the kingdom of heaven."[29] Considering ourselves rich in spirit is a self-satisfied path to dangerous, spiritual poverty. When we adopt the humbling attitude that we are poor in spirit, regardless of our circumstances, we are admitting that we are dependent upon God for all that is good and necessary in our lives. The Lord has been aware of our deadly tendency to forget Him in our untroubled and secure lives since the beginnings of His people.

In Deuteronomy 8:7–18, the Lord told Israel that He was bringing them into a good land of abundant water, wheat, figs, olives, and iron. However, He cautioned them to take care so they would not forget Him and become proud when they experienced prosperity in this land of abundance. He reminded them that He alone had brought them out of slavery and led them through "the great and terrifying wilderness." Thus, He warned them not to be

---

29. Matthew 5:3.

lifted up in their hearts and say, "My power and the might of my hand have gotten me this wealth."

Because the Lord loves us, He will do what He must to keep us from being at ease and inattentive. Therefore, if you are a Christian, it is helpful to know that the Father at times wants you to be uncomfortable, uneasy, and unsure. No, He doesn't want you to be unsure of your salvation, His grace or love, but He does want you to be uncomfortable enough in your life so that you will turn to Him and learn to trust Him when, in His sovereign wisdom, He considers that necessary for your good.

The Lord May Challenge Our Understanding of Spirituality

One of the ways the Lord may upset our comfort is by interjecting a supernatural challenge into our lives to test if we fully love Him. Consider what He told Israel: "If a prophet or a dreamer of dreams arises among you and gives you a sign or a wonder, and the sign or wonder that he tells you comes to pass, and if he says, 'Let us go after other gods,' which you have not known, 'and let us serve them,' you shall not listen to the words of that prophet or that dreamer of dreams. For the LORD your God is testing you, to know whether you love the LORD your God with all your heart and with all your soul."[30]

This passage tells us that the Lord will allow false prophets and visionaries to perform signs and wonders and accurately foretell the future in order to test His people to determine if they love Him with all their hearts. Do we desire a spiritual life that is rooted in a profoundly deep relationship with God, or one that pursues every new spiritual event or prophet that comes down the road? I believe this is one area where some Christians have gone awry. I understand the glorious experiences people sometimes have when the Lord saves them, fills them with His Spirit, or manifests His presence. I know the wondrous reality of seeing individuals

---

30. Deuteronomy 13:1–3.

dramatically impacted by the miraculous works of God. However, we deceive ourselves if we think this is the daily norm for spiritual life, and the error has been to pursue such things in an attempt to insure their continuation and thereby somehow prove that we are living exciting supernatural lives. We may become bored with a life where dramatic spiritual events are often absent and seek to recapture them. Thus, we become dissatisfied, to our detriment, with a life that should be defined, not with continual thrilling events, but with a humbling and remarkable relationship with the Lord of all that exists. This error has led sincere believers into many strange beliefs and practices. We should not forget Jesus' blistering renunciation of such seeking: "An evil and adulterous generation seeks for a sign, but no sign will be given to it except the sign of the prophet Jonah."[31] Jonah was the distressing foreshadowing of a Man to come who would die a terrible death and come back from the dead. Our primary emphasis should always be Jesus and His sacrificial death and conquering resurrection. Be forewarned. The Lord will test you "to know whether you love the LORD your God with all your heart and with all your soul" by permitting false prophets and visionaries to perform signs and wonders. He will threaten your perceived understanding of spirituality for your spiritual good.

The Lord May Allow Deprivation

Through Amos, a prophet to Israel, the Lord said that He would send rain to one city and not to another and that "one field would have rain, and the field on which it did not rain would wither."[32]

If you were an Israelite who was cultivating a drought-ridden field, yet knew of some land down the road on which it had rained, what would you think? Would you wonder if the Lord favored that farmer over you? You had worked as hard as he had, if not harder. Why the other family and not yours? The Lord tells us why

---

31. Matthew 12:39.
32. Amos 4:6–8.

The God of Discomfort

He caused His people to experience lack: so they would return to Him. You may think, "These things wouldn't happen to me. I'm a Christian, and I believe in Jesus and follow Him. I don't need to return to Him." Be very careful. Your status as a Christian believer may not be in doubt, but remember that the Lord told His chosen people that He would test them to determine if they loved the Lord their God with all their hearts and with all their souls. Is it possible that you do not love Him as wholly as you should? Of course it is. No human being is able to keep perfectly the first and greatest commandment of the Law: "You shall love the LORD your God with all your heart and with all your soul and with all your might."[33]

Your loving Father would rather you suffer discomfort than live a life of pallid complacency, lacking tenacious adoration for Him. His application of deprivation to your life so you will know Him better is an act of grace and love.

Perhaps you are aware of this admonition from the book of Hebrews, in which the author told believers, "It is for discipline that you have to endure. God is treating you as sons. For what son is there whom his father does not discipline? If you are left without discipline, in which all have participated, then you are illegitimate children and not sons."[34]

These verses tell us that it is a certainty that our heavenly Father will discipline us. In fact, if we are not disciplined, it is an indication that we are not His children.

A doctor, out of necessity, may need to re-break a patient's leg so that it will heal properly. Is the doctor evil, inattentive, or attempting to make his patient's life more difficult by inflicting additional pain? No, the physician knows what must be done in order to heal the injury. Although Christians have become God's children through re-birth, He loves them and wants what is best for their spiritual lives, and that will require what may be considered painful discipline. Are you a son or daughter of the Lord God Almighty? If you are, welcome to the fellowship of the God of discomfort.

33. Deuteronomy 6:5.
34. Hebrews 12:7–8.

Prophets Poking Their Fingers in Our Chests

If the previous scriptural examples are not sufficient to convince us that God's will is for us to be sometimes ill at ease, let's look at what the Lord, through Paul, told the believers in Corinth. Twice he exhorted them to earnestly desire to prophesy.[35] Why would that make a Christian uncomfortable? Because we know what prophets did in Scripture. In the Old Testament, their bony fingers were continually poking Israel or Judah in their chests, demanding that they abandon their idols and unholy military alliances, trust only in the Lord, and return in obedience to Him. Prophets were often foretellers of misfortune because of the unrepentant sinfulness of God's people.

We see in the Gospels that Jesus Himself was a prophet, and that aspect of His ministry was similarly set about with thorns. He did not win followers from the religious community when He told the Pharisees that the devil was their father.[36] Jesus did not make Himself popular by informing the Jewish authorities that they were hypocritical leaders who were clean on the outside but filthy on the inside[37] and that for the sake of their tradition they had made void the Word of God.[38] He did not spread sunshine, joy, and promises of prosperity when He declared that Jerusalem and the temple would one day be destroyed.[39] In the book of Revelation, Jesus reprimanded the church at Ephesus for leaving their first love and commanded that they repent.[40] He alerted the church at Smyrna that they were soon going to suffer, and some would be thrown into prison. "Do not fear what you are about to suffer. Behold, the devil is about to throw some of you into prison, that

---

35. 1 Corinthians 14:1, 39.
36. John 8:44.
37. Matthew 23:25.
38. Matthew 15:1–12.
39. Luke 19:41–44; Matthew 24:1–2.
40. Revelation 2:4.

you may be tested, and for ten days you will have tribulation. Be faithful unto death, and I will give you the crown of life."[41]

He warned the church at Pergamum that He would war against those who held to destructive teaching and demanded that they repent.[42] He announced to the church at Thyatira that He would cast one of their women into a sickbed, and those committing adultery with her into great tribulation, insisting on their repentance.[43] He rebuked the church at Sardis for being spiritually dead and called them to repent.[44] He told the church at Laodicea that although they thought they were rich and prosperous, they were, instead, "wretched, pitiable, poor, blind, and naked," again charging them to repent.[45]

Jesus is our Savior and Lord, but He is also a fierce prophet of discomfort.

Like Him, and by His Spirit, believers in the New Testament were called to the office of prophet. Agabus prophesied disastrous news about a coming famine.[46] He also warned Paul, after binding his own feet and hands with Paul's belt, that "This is how the Jews at Jerusalem will bind the man who owns this belt and deliver him into the hands of the Gentiles."[47] Paul foretold misfortune and loss when he warned the centurion, pilot, and ship owner not to sail to Crete.[48] He may have lost some friends when he informed the believers at Galatia that they were deceived, and he wished the Judaizers who were troubling them would emasculate themselves.[49] Paul may have offended some Corinthians when he wrote that they were infants and fleshly for preferring certain Christian personalities

---

41. Revelation 2:10.
42. Revelation 2:14–16.
43. Revelation 2:20–22.
44. Revelation 3:2.
45. Revelation 3:17–19.
46. Acts 11:28.
47. Acts 21:11b.
48. Acts 27:10–26.
49. Galatians 5:12.

over others[50] or when he notified them that they were weak and sick because they were not discerning the body of Christ.[51] Did Christians consider Paul a preacher of gloom and doom when he foretold that perilous times would come in the last days?[52] Jude wrote a fiery letter about ungodly people who had crept into the Church. Peter issued a similar warning in his second letter.[53]

Prophets are called by God to make His people uncomfortable and repentant, while foretelling the consequences of their rebellion. Therefore, when the Lord exhorts us to earnestly desire to prophesy, He is informing us that it is His will for a measure of discomfort to be present in our fellowships, perhaps a very large measure. He wants His bold, disrupting voice to be heard in our midst.

Does God like to stir up trouble? Yes, and He has a glorious reason: He loves us. He knows how prone we are to sinful complacency and self-satisfaction. Status quo is our default human setting. It does not take long for His children to think they have this Christian thing figured out, switch on the go-easy spiritual autopilot, and turn our attention to other things. This false contentment is the result of our sinful condition, of which our loving God is very aware. It is the reason, as we know, that we need a Savior who died for our sins. Therefore, we continually need to be brought up short so we can repent of our complacency, sin, or ignorance, ask for forgiveness, and move on in maturity.

Prophecy Strengthens and Comforts Believers

The ultimate driver for prophetic utterances in the Church is God's love for His people. Prophecy provokes and convicts, revealing

---

50. 1 Corinthians 3:1–4.
51. 1 Corinthians 11: 27–32.
52. 2 Timothy 3:1–9.
53. 2 Peter 2:1–22.

the secrets of one's heart[54] but ultimately builds up the believer[55] because the Lord will inevitably fulfill His great and precious promises, although tough discipline may be required. An example of this contrast is in Isaiah 48:18-19. Here, the Lord is grieving through the prophet about the upcoming judgment: "Oh that you had paid attention to my commandments! Then your peace would have been like a river, and your righteousness like the waves of the sea; your offspring would have been like the sand, and your descendants like its grains; their name would never be cut off or destroyed from before me."

However, in the very next chapter, the Lord spoke these delightful words of joy, comfort, and care: "Sing for joy, O heavens, and exult, O earth; break forth, O mountains, into singing! For the LORD has comforted his people and will have compassion on his afflicted. But Zion said, 'The LORD has forsaken me; my Lord has forgotten me.' Can a woman forget her nursing child, that she should have no compassion on the son of her womb? Even these may forget, yet I will not forget you. Behold, I have engraved you on the palms of my hands; your walls are continually before me."[56]

The Lord our God is a God of discomfort. However, He is also the God of compassion, comfort, and inevitable victory. He will bring His repentant people to overwhelming triumph, though the road may be spiny and steep.[57]

Share in Suffering

Paul told Timothy, "Share in suffering as a good soldier of Christ Jesus. No soldier gets entangled in civilian pursuits, since his aim is to please the one who enlisted him."[58] How does one do that? There is only one answer, and we will not find it in a book entitled *Ten*

---

54. 1 Corinthians 14:24-25.
55. 1 Corinthians 14:3-5.
56. Isaiah 49:13-16.
57. Romans 8:35-39.
58. 2 Timothy 2:3-4.

Ways to Live as a Good, Suffering Soldier of Jesus. Setting up a list of laws or, rather, principles, as we like to call them, is misguided. That will only lead to self-satisfied and self-righteous legalism. No, we will find the how-to as we seek Him and read His Word. He is, after all, the way, the truth, and the life. He knows how to live this way and will tell us.

However, as uncomfortable as it may be to suffer as a soldier in God's kingdom, there is richness here. Jesus told the Laodiceans, "I counsel you to buy from me gold refined by fire, so that you may be rich."[59] When Jesus said this, He did not mean that if believers entered the refining flames and thereby suffered loss, that there would be a payoff at the end with more earthly affluence. He was talking about spiritual abundance to a church, which by virtue of its material prosperity, considered itself rich when it was actually quite poor. This is the one who said, "Sell your possessions, and give to the needy. Provide yourselves with moneybags that do not grow old, with a treasure in the heavens that does not fail, where no thief approaches and no moth destroys. For where your treasure is, there will your heart be also."[60]

This is a challenging command in a culture that extols worldly fortune. However, we must keep in mind that our God is a consuming fire,[61] not a campfire for roasting marshmallows. Jesus' unyielding desire is that we possess wealth in the heavens, not store up what could be spiritually dangerous treasure on earth, although that accumulated affluence may offer greater temporary, physical comfort. Our wealth in heaven is true treasure—true, eternal riches indeed.

The Discomfort of Transience

Laurie and I once taught English to a family from the Karen tribe of Burma that had immigrated to the United States. They had lived

---

59. Revelation 3:18a.
60. Luke 12:33–34.
61. Hebrews 12:29.

for thirteen years in a refugee camp in Thailand. When the father was a child, his family had been attacked, and he ran into the jungle for safety. Tragically, he never saw his parents or siblings again. This family's experience is just one in our world's long history rife with heartbreaking accounts of people groups that have been uprooted from their native lands, dispersed, or forced into settlement or refugee camps. Time and space will not allow us to adequately recount these tragic events, some of which are occurring at the time of this writing. However, if we investigate Scripture, we will see that God's people, both individually and nationally, became displaced persons more than once.

Moses, exiled from Egypt, considered himself a stranger in a strange land.[62]

The Northern Kingdom was conquered by the Assyrians and dispersed because they had egregiously sinned against the Lord by worshiping other gods and setting up for themselves "pillars and Asherim on every high hill and under every green tree."[63]

Judah, the Southern Kingdom, was taken captive to Babylon because they had been "exceedingly unfaithful, following all the abominations of the nations." They had mocked "the messengers of God," despised His words, and scoffed at his prophets.[64]

The Lord allowed the Diaspora of Israel and the captivity of Judah because His people had worshiped idols and turned away from Him. They thus became foreigners in lands not their own. He removed them from their ancestral home because He loved them and desired what was best for them: to love, know, and obey Him.

A Reminder of Uncomfortable Transience: The Feast of Booths

Israel's celebration of the Feast of Booths is an instructive example of how the Lord reminded His people of their need for an abiding

---

62. Exodus 2:21–22.
63. 2 Kings 17:5–12.
64. 2 Chronicles 36:14–16.

sense of uncomfortable transience. He did not simply think this was a good idea—He commanded it: "You shall dwell in booths for seven days. All native Israelites shall dwell in booths, that your generations may know that I made the people of Israel dwell in booths when I brought them out of the land of Egypt: I am the Lord your God."[65]

The people of Israel needed to be reminded that there was a time when they had no permanent dwelling place. I believe one of the reasons the Lord established this annual feast was to challenge Israel's tendency to give in to a self-contentment in what He had given them—the Land of Promise, flowing with milk and honey. After what their forefathers had experienced as slaves in Egypt, living freely and abundantly as the chosen nation of God was another day in Paradise in comparison.

Christians, Transients All

In the New Testament, God's people are referred to as strangers and exiles: "These all died in faith, not having received the things promised, but having seen them and greeted them from afar, and having acknowledged that they were strangers and exiles on the earth."[66]

The idea that God's people are temporary residents on earth still exists as a stream of thought among Western Christians, but it seems to have been reduced to a trickle. Songs that echo the theme of the song, *This World Is Not My Home*, seem to have been reduced to whispers. Our materialistic, this-world-is-all-there-is culture speaks with a very loud voice. Nevertheless, the impermanent condition for the Lord's sinful-but-forgiven loved ones has been His heart throughout Scripture.

---

65. Leviticus 23:42–43.
66. Hebrews 11:13.

The City of Man and the City of God

One of the themes of the Bible is the contrast of the city of man to the city of God. We are told not to love this temporary, worldly city—"Do not love the world or the things in the world. If anyone loves the world, the love of the Father is not in him"[67]—but to seek a spiritual, eternal one. The author of Hebrews wrote that men and women of faith "desire a better country, that is, a heavenly one. Therefore God is not ashamed to be called their God, for he has prepared for them a city," "whose designer and builder is God."[68] There will be comfort, peace, glory, and apparently, some kind of inclusive rulership there.[69]

We see those two cities in most vivid contrast in the book of Revelation. The city of man, Babylon, represented as a prostitute in chapter 17:1–5, is eventually destroyed.[70] However, the wondrous city of God is established afterwards. "And I saw the holy city, new Jerusalem, coming down out of heaven from God, prepared as a bride adorned for her husband. And I heard a loud voice from the throne saying, 'Behold, the dwelling place of God is with man. He will dwell with them, and they will be his people, and God himself will be with them as their God. He will wipe away every tear from their eyes, and death shall be no more, neither shall there be mourning, nor crying, nor pain anymore, for the former things have passed away.'"[71]

The New Jerusalem is the place of eternal residency that awaits us. Therefore, while we are living in and under the influence of the temporary city of man, it is necessary that we are continually challenged to walk by faith in our magnificent God and not according to the dark, burdensome, yet attractive reality of what the world presents. In the passage that follows, we will find Paul telling the Corinthians that although there will be distress in this life, an

---

67. 1 John 2:15.
68. Hebrews 11:16, 10b.
69. Revelation 7:17; 21:4; 5:9–10; 22:3–5.
70. Revelation 18:10, 19.
71. Revelation 21:2–4.

eternal, not temporal, hope awaits. "For this light momentary affliction is preparing for us an eternal weight of glory beyond all comparison, as we look not to the things that are seen but to the things that are unseen. For the things that are seen are transient, but the things that are unseen are eternal. For we know that if the tent that is our earthly home is destroyed, we have a building from God, a house not made with hands, eternal in the heavens."[72]

These are profound verses. However, its encouraging promise is an answer to the reality of earthly hardship and affliction. Does God allow suffering? Yes. Does He even cause it? Yes. This is His purpose and plan to bring us into a future that is eternally glorious beyond all comparison. We do not see it that way and are often quite unsure we want it. However, in spite of our uncertainty and even at times, blatant unfaithfulness, He desires what is best for us, although discomfort awaits. In our ignorance, we prefer a comfortable life with no weight of everlasting glory; a limping walk on a broken leg that impedes our anemic journey instead of a re-broken, healed one that allows us to summit the mountains of eternity.

This is the God of discomforting love, peace, sacrifice, and victory.

This is the God we do not know.

---

72. 2 Corinthians 4:17—5:1.

3

The God of Dust and Glory

*But we have this treasure in jars of clay,
to show that the surpassing power
belongs to God and not to us.*[1]

∽ Paul to the church at Corinth

EVERY DAY, ALL OVER the world, wondrous creations of God die, fall to the earth or the bottom of the sea, and decay. Petunias and Plumeria. Jellyfish. Antelopes, hummingbirds, and caterpillars. Each of these organisms is so complex and beautiful that humankind cannot duplicate them. However, the Lord created them all out of nothing with His extravagant, imaginative power. Yet, in spite of their splendor and intricacies, we are not overly concerned when they are destroyed. Fallen flowers are walked upon. Animals and birds that die in the wild simply rot where they lie. Most of us have no qualms about a crushed insect on our windshields, yet that moth or mayfly is so magnificent a creation that it would require millions of dollars to manufacture just one robotic facsimile. Even if such a thing were possible, that machine would not possess the ability to sustain itself or procreate. It would have no self-existent

---

1. 2 Corinthians 4:7.

life. Human beings simply cannot replicate even the most common things that God has created: A leaf. A seed.

God's creations are extraordinary yet quite ordinary—an inscrutable mix of realities.

We find this to be true of us, as well. Human beings are extraordinary—the pinnacle of God's creation. Of all that He made, only we were fashioned by His own hand. Man is the only one of the Lord's living creations into whom He breathed the breath of life.[2] God proclaimed everything that He created very good, but people are the most precious of all of His handiwork. We know this beyond question because He Himself died to redeem the sinful children of Adam and bring them into His family and kingdom. Yet, we are also very common. He formed us from the dust of the ground.

God Glorifies Himself in His Creation

In His wisdom, the Lord God Almighty has chosen to glorify Himself through all that He has created. The heavens offer spectacular evidence of God's work, masterpieces of energy, mass, and light that astound and baffle us. King David proclaimed, "The heavens declare the glory of God, and the sky above proclaims his handiwork."[3] What rises up in you when you behold a beautiful sunset or sunrise? When you see a photo taken by a deep sky telescope of millions of not only stars but galaxies, do you experience a sense of wonder that is difficult to express? All of it was created by, through, and for Jesus from nothing.[4] All of us know that it is simply beyond our capability to manufacture even a lifeless moon, much less a blazing sun. Only God can do such things, and He is therefore glorified in these magnificent, imponderable wonders.

Concerning God's work through people, however, they alone among the Lord's creations choose to take God's glory to

---

2. Genesis 2:7.
3. Psalm 19:1.
4. Colossians 1:15–17.

themselves, which stars and starfish cannot do. Unlike us, everything else in the world behaves according to its design and thus glorifies the Lord. Seedlings fiercely press past clods of soil, seeking the sun as they thrust roots downward to find water. Lions and sharks ferociously and mercilessly kill their prey, as God created them to do. Monarch butterflies, with fragile wings and tiny bodies, using a divinely installed magnetic compass and a sensor to determine the position of the sun, obediently flutter 3,000 miles to warmer climes. Bees are made to manufacture honey, somehow, and pollinate flowers. We alone are the disobedient, taking-glory-for-ourselves ones, and therefore He must make it crystal clear that it is His hand at work through us, not ours. Scripture teems with examples of the Lord doing mighty acts in which His people participate but exert little if any influence or power.

Moses

What power did Moses wield when Israel crossed the Red Sea?

He held up his staff.[5]

Moses did do something in faith. But was it Moses' power and a piece of wood that parted the water? After Israel had passed over on dry ground and Pharaoh's army had been destroyed, this is what Moses and Israel sang, giving praise to the only One who can perform such feats:

> I will sing to the LORD,
> for he has triumphed gloriously;
> the horse and his rider he has thrown into the sea.
> The LORD is my strength and my song,
> and he has become my salvation;
> this is my God, and I will praise him,
> my father's God, and I will exalt him.
> The LORD is a man of war; the LORD is his name
> (Exodus 15:1b–3).

---

5. Exodus 14:15–16, 21.

Truly, what else would one sing after seeing and experiencing this event?

He alone is God. We are not.

He is the King and Sovereign over all things. We are not.

He has all the power—all of it. We do not.

God gave Israel victory over the Amalekites because Moses held up his hands. Whenever he lowered them, the enemy of Israel prevailed.[6]

Yes, Israel fought. But it was God, through His power, not the height of Moses' weakening arms or Israel's military might, who caused His people to triumph.

Did the Lord need Moses to perform these acts? No. Could He have caused the sea to stand up in heaps without Moses' involvement? Of course. Could He have destroyed the hostile army of the Amalekites without Moses' aid? Yes. Why, then, did the most powerful being in the universe choose these courses of action? It was to let Israel know—to let us all know—that He is the great Deliverer, the supreme Actor in human events, and He and He alone does mighty deeds. We have the awesome privilege of witnessing them and sometimes participating in them.

Joshua

Joshua and the people of Israel were moving into and conquering the land that God promised. Before them lay the seemingly impregnable city of Jericho, protected by immense walls. However, the Lord had a plan to bring down this great place, and that plan did not include catapults, siege works, or fire. It included marching, shouting, and the blowing of trumpets. Israel did as God instructed.[7]

The people of Israel obeyed the Lord in faith. However, was it because of the marching, the trumpet blowing, and the shouting

---

6. Exodus 17:10–13.
7. Joshua 6:15–16, 20.

that the walls fell? No, only our almighty God has the power to collapse the walls of a fortified, enemy city, without the aid of men.

David

Did David think that his skill or war craft gave him victory over his enemies? Although he fought with sling, sword, and shield, he stood before Goliath and boldly proclaimed, "This day the LORD will deliver you into my hand, and I will strike you down and cut off your head. And I will give the dead bodies of the host of the Philistines this day to the birds of the air and to the wild beasts of the earth, that all the earth may know that there is a God in Israel, and that all this assembly may know that the LORD saves not with sword and spear. For the battle is the LORD's, and he will give you into our hand."[8]

God brings victory. We, stunning creations of loam and loess, cannot. We may fight with every weapon imaginable, but unless He wills it, we are fighting in vain. The battle, as David declared, is the Lord's.

Gideon

God caused an army of Midianite warriors to turn and fight against each other when Gideon and his small army of one hundred men blew trumpets and smashed jars.[9] Who except the Lord of the universe would use this tactical strategy in battle? In truth, we are the shattered jars: broken, precious creations God employs to glorify Himself as He alone brings overwhelming victory against forces arrayed against Him and His people.

---

8. 1 Samuel 17:46–47.
9. Judges 7:19–23.

Hezekiah

When Hezekiah was king, he was in danger of being attacked by a massive Assyrian army, and he cried out to God. Through the prophet Isaiah, the Lord answered the worried king: "Therefore thus says the LORD concerning the king of Assyria: He shall not come into this city or shoot an arrow there, or come before it with a shield or cast up a siege mound against it. By the way that he came, by the same he shall return, and he shall not come into this city, declares the LORD. For I will defend this city to save it, for my own sake and for the sake of my servant David."[10]

This is what happened: "And that night the angel of the LORD went out and struck down 185,000 in the camp of the Assyrians. And when people arose early in the morning, behold, these were all dead bodies. Then Sennacherib king of Assyria departed and went home and lived at Nineveh."[11]

Hezekiah implored God for deliverance, but he and his soldiers, wondrous concoctions of clay, did absolutely nothing to win this contest. This account notifies us about a glorious Victor who was yet to come, who would defeat our enemies for us. Must we pray? Yes. However, we do so in the knowledge that our warfare is not against flesh and blood.[12] It is a spiritual battle against spiritual forces, which Jesus alone is able to conquer.

God Is Glorified Through Believers

Let's look at the New Testament. Here are two of the most explicit examples when Christian men made it undeniably clear that it was the Lord at work and not themselves. The first is when the Lord, through the ministry of Peter, healed the lame man at the Beautiful Gate. Peter asked, "Men of Israel, why do you wonder at this, or why do you stare at us, as though by our own power or piety we

---

10. 2 Kings 19:32–34.
11. 2 Kings 19:35–36.
12. Ephesians 6:12.

have made him walk?"[13] Peter, an apostle called by Jesus Himself, knew he was only a vessel of earth and that he had healed no one. Our compassionate Jesus restored this poor man.

Paul

In the city of Lystra, the Lord cured another lame man through the apostle Paul. The inhabitants wanted to offer sacrifices to Paul and Barnabas, believing they were gods. However, Paul shouted: "Men, why are you doing these things? We also are men, of like nature with you, and we bring you good news, that you should turn from these vain things to a living God, who made the heaven and the earth and the sea and all that is in them."[14]

Paul attempted to make it clear that they were only men, of like nature with those who erroneously wanted to exalt Barnabas and him as gods. Only our gracious God, who provides good things to all, healed this broken individual. He alone was to receive the praise for this miraculous event.

More Than Children: Temples

Believers in Jesus are children of their heavenly Father, but after Jesus ascended and the Holy Spirit was poured out at Pentecost, the bodies of Christian believers also became the very temples of God. This was always part of the Lord's outlandish new-covenant plan. Since human beings are sinful, it was necessary that these earthly temples be made holy and pure. Thus, by the blood of Jesus, holy God incarnate, men and women are cleansed so they might become the dwelling places of God Himself. The Lord Almighty has now taken up residence in temples not made by the fallen hands of man, but by the hand of God.[15]

---

13. Acts 3:12.
14. Acts 14:15.
15. 1 Corinthians 3:16–17; 6:18–20; Ephesians 2:19–22.

How glorious is this human temple? Glorious indeed. As we saw earlier, the Lord created these amazing genetic wonders out of dirt in the likeness of Himself. We are the crown of His creation. Yet, Paul tells us: "For God, who said, 'Let light shine out of darkness,' has shone in our hearts to give the light of the knowledge of the glory of God in the face of Jesus Christ. But we have this treasure in jars of clay, to show that the surpassing power belongs to God and not to us."[16]

The container for the treasure of God is as complex as anything He created but as unremarkable as the dust of the ground. The surpassing power that was necessary for this extraordinary reality belongs to God and not to us.

Crumbles of Common Dirt

God inhabits living, breathing, crumbles of common dirt, but He is holy—set apart from His creation in ways that we find difficult to understand. Holy and lowly—an unfathomable tumble of ideas from the remarkable mind of God. We can bring forth nothing without Him. Great basketball players do not manipulate their genes in their mother's wombs so they will grow tall and gifted in the game. A physicist, squirming as a fetus, does not build a brain capable of understanding quantum mechanics. Unborn singers do not create vocal chords that can effortlessly trill through multiple octaves without a flattened note. All that we carve or cast, all that we have wrought or written, finds its origin in Him.

He is the God of dust and glory.

He is the God we do not know.

---

16. 2 Corinthians 4:6–7.

4

The God Who Is Perfect

*Can you explain why lightning flashes
at the orders of God who knows all things?
Or how he hangs the clouds in empty space?*[1]

~ The Lord questions Job

MUCH OF MANKIND SEEMS to be on the relentless pursuit of perfection. We want to be perfect parents with perfect children, and in perfect relationships with our spouses, after we have had perfect weddings and then move into stunningly perfect homes.

However, is perfection really possible?

Voltaire wrote, "Perfection is attained by slow degrees; it requires the hand of time."[2] However, most of us, no matter how much time passes, realize that perfection is not possible. In spite of our best intentions, we make mistakes—and let's be honest—we make a lot of them. However, there is one who did not need to summit the peak of faultless excellence. He has always been perfect, is now, and will be forever. The sluggish hand of time was not needed for Him to evolve to that state. Moses sang this amazing tribute about Him thousands of years ago:

1. Job 37:15–16 CEV.
2. Day, *Collacon: Prose Quotations*, 671 s.v. "Patience."

The God We Do Not Know

> Give ear, O heavens, and I will speak,
> and let the earth hear the words of my mouth.
> May my teaching drop as the rain,
> my speech distill as the dew,
> like gentle rain upon the tender grass,
> and like showers upon the herb.
> For I will proclaim the name of the Lord;
> ascribe greatness to our God!
> The Rock, his work is perfect,
> for all his ways are justice.
> A God of faithfulness and without iniquity,
> just and upright is he. (Deuteronomy 32:1–4).

God is perfect. There is absolutely no flaw in Him or His works whatsoever and never will be—for eternity. It is impossible for us to make a similar claim about our accomplishments that is not laughable because we cannot create eternal things that will not decay or become useless, let alone be subject to divine scrutiny, time without end. Only the Lord, almighty God of the universe, is capable, is strong, is wise enough to do this. He is at work even as you read this, doing wondrous, ageless, matchless things, which the Bible says He alone can do.[3]

God's Perfect Knowledge

Not only is God's work perfect, His knowledge is perfect.

When I think about the immensity of His creation, my mind turns to blazing stars, titanic mountains, and the astonishing diversity of all living things. However, I do not usually consider the underlying principles of creation: why things are the way they are. Not only did the Lord create the trillions of burning suns in the universe, He brought into existence—out of nothing—the physics that make them work—that make everything work, with

---

3. Psalm 72:18.

The God Who Is Perfect

perfection: time, space, motion, mass, light, gravity, and energy. He did not borrow these ideas or spin them off from a pre-existing notion of reality from another source. No gods existed before Him.[4] He fashioned all that exists, by Himself, alone.

Not only did He create these flawless principles and laws in and by which we live, He created knowledge itself. The concept of knowledge as we know it would not even exist if He had not created it. There is nothing our Father does not know. It is impossible that anything exists or is at work on the earth or in the universe of which He is unaware. For finite human beings, such power of mind is an impossibility. A person ten thousand times as brilliant as Einstein will never possess it. A man may acquire more knowledge than any living individual; however, he is not aware of every swallow that flutters and falls to the earth. However, God is mindful of them all.[5]

Astonishingly, God "determines the number of the stars; he gives to all of them their names."[6] Scientists tell us that there are approximately one hundred billion stars in our Milky Way galaxy alone and ten trillion galaxies in the universe. These are rough estimates. No one has actually counted them. So, using the Milky Way as a galactic benchmark, if we were to multiply these two figures in order to determine—again, roughly—the number of stars in the universe, it would be a one with twenty-four zeroes after it—a number we simply cannot comprehend.

Not only does our almighty God know the names and number of the stars, He is aware of the words in our mouths before we speak them. King David wrote of this and confessed, "Such knowledge is too wonderful for me; it is high; I cannot attain it."[7] In his prayer at the dedication of the temple, Solomon proclaimed that the Lord knew "the hearts of all the children of mankind."[8] If that were not enough to prove our God possesses all-encompassing

---

4. Isaiah 43:10.
5. Matthew 10:29–31.
6. Psalm 147:4.
7. Psalm 139:6.
8. 1 Kings 8:39b.

knowledge—and it really is, wouldn't you agree—He knew the names of His people before the foundation of the world and wrote them in a book.[9] If you are a believer in Jesus Christ, your name was written down in the Lamb's book of life before the earth on which you were born even existed.

This is the God who exhausts our comprehension.

This is the God we do not know.

God's Strength Is Perfect

Long ago and far away, when I led children's praise time, we sang a song proclaiming that God was so great and mighty that He could do anything. A simple song, but these children were declaring a strong, biblical truth. There is nothing the Lord God Almighty cannot do. The greatest king of Israel, David, was not shy in his praise of His boundless might:

> The voice of the LORD flashes forth flames of fire.
>
> The voice of the LORD shakes the wilderness;
>
> the LORD shakes the wilderness of Kadesh.
>
> The voice of the LORD makes the deer give birth
>
> and strips the forests bare, and in his temple
>
> all cry, "Glory!" (Psalm 29:7–9).

The Lord God is supremely strong. Nothing exists over which He does not exert absolute sovereignty. Nothing happens on the earth or in the universe unless He causes or allows it. If another, superior power existed, He would not be God. No gods are beside Him and none will reign after Him.[10] When He acts, no spiritual or earthly might will come along and usurp what He has done, unless He permits it.

The Lord God thought up all the concepts of strength with which we are familiar. The symbols for earthly power we employ are based upon that which He designed: Lions, tigers, bears, elephants,

---

9. Revelation 17:8.
10. Isaiah 45:21.

and eagles. Tornadoes, hurricanes, earthquakes, and storms are arranged and controlled by Him, their Creator. Remarkably, every lightning bolt is directed by the Lord: "He covers his hands with the lightning and commands it to strike the mark."[11] All that we know of might came from His mind.

Asking Questions About God's Great Power

However, the Lord does not often speak of His immense potency, which is explicitly revealed in His creation and supernatural works. He simply acts—and those actions speak for themselves. He expects us to understand that obvious reality; however, too often we do not. Therefore, He challenges our inability to grasp His indisputable, sovereign strength by asking questions, as He did to Job: "Where were you when I laid the foundation of the earth? Tell me, if you have understanding."[12] He asked a similar question of Abraham and Sarah when she laughed at His improbable prophecy concerning her upcoming pregnancy: "Is anything too hard for the LORD? At the appointed time I will return to you, about this time next year, and Sarah shall have a son."[13]

If you are familiar with this astounding story, that is precisely what happened. Enabling an old man and woman to conceive at a predicted time was not too difficult for Him.

The Lord put the same rhetorical question to Jeremiah when the prophet expressed incredulity at God's command to buy a field at Anathoth, a town about three miles north of Jerusalem, even though Jerusalem had been conquered and given into the hands of the Chaldeans.[14] The Lord responded with this question: "Behold, I am the LORD, the God of all flesh. Is anything too hard for me?"[15] He then told Jeremiah what He was going to do and why it was safe

---

11. Job 36:32.
12. Job 38:4.
13. Genesis 18:14.
14. Jeremiah 32:24–25.
15. Jeremiah 32:27.

for him to purchase property: He would bring His people back to Israel.[16] Jeremiah could not see it, but the Lord had the power to do exactly what He said He would do, as history bears witness.

The wise answer to God's faith-challenging questions is, "No, there is nothing too difficult for You, Lord." All things—creating and upholding all that exists, healing broken bodies and lives, and conquering death and sin forever—are possible for Him.

God knows all things. He can do all things. His works, knowledge, and unmovable might are . . . perfect.

God Tells the Truth Perfectly

Every word of God is true, Proverbs 30:5 tells us—every word. He speaks with absolute precision. He and He alone knows the eternal truth in any and all situations. Therefore, if we want to know the truth, we go to Him and the revelation of Him in His Word. When He tells us that we are re-birthed sons and daughters of God who are greatly loved by Him, that is an eternal certainty. When He states that if we do not know the Son we are condemned, that is the way it is and always will be. His words are authentic in the deepest, most meaningful, eternal way possible. The Lord God is not lying about these things. He cannot lie.[17]

When Jesus said, "I am the way, and the truth, and the life. No one comes to the Father except through me,"[18] He was stating an unqualified fact. He really is the only way to eternal life with God. For Jesus to say that He is the way to the Father and His home, it means that He knows everything about what is required to arrive at that eternal destination. He embodied that road, in fact. Another pathway does not exist elsewhere, and no one else could reveal it to us. In addition, when Jesus says He is the truth, He is pronouncing that He is the root core of all spiritual knowledge. No verifiable certainty is obtainable outside of who He Himself is. Finally, when

---

16. Jeremiah 32:36–39.
17. Titus 1:2; Hebrews 6:18.
18. John 14:6.

The God Who Is Perfect

Jesus asserts that He is the life, He is proclaiming that all that is necessary for life is in Him; is Him, in fact. No other life, as defined by the One who was and is life itself, is available apart from Him.

God Keeps His Promises Perfectly

While God's people should endeavor to keep their promises, we quickly discover that all too often we are dreadfully unable to do so. Although we may lift our voices in song proclaiming, "I will always love and serve You, Lord," we should probably sing, "Lord, please help me love and serve You—and forgive me when I don't." Israel and the Church did not, do not, and cannot remain faithful to the vows they make to God. Through Hosea, the Lord said, "What shall I do with you, O Ephraim? What shall I do with you, O Judah? Your love is like a morning cloud, like the dew that goes early away."[19]

Let us be honest. In spite of our best intentions, our love for God is as fleeting as the morning dew.

We must be ready to confess that we are tragically unable to keep the first commandment to love our God, or any other of the moral and spiritual requirements of the Old Covenant. That's why a new one was necessary, one in which the covenant keeper is God, not us. He is able to keep His promises—for eternity.

The Gospels are brimming with promises Jesus made. Here is just one powerful example: "Let not your hearts be troubled. Believe in God; believe also in me. In my Father's house are many rooms. If it were not so, would I have told you that I go to prepare a place for you? And if I go and prepare a place for you, I will come again and will take you to myself, that where I am you may be also. And you know the way to where I am going."[20]

This promise from the God who only tells the truth has great significance for Christians, if they should ever come to doubt that they possess eternal life. In faith, we would believe that God did

---

19. Hosea 6:4.
20. John 14:1–4.

not lie about His people living forever. Jesus Himself has gone to prepare a place for us. He said He will come again. He said He will take us to Himself, so we can be where He is. This is not simply a pleasant thought painted on a coffee cup. It is a guarantee from the God who keeps every promise He has ever made. If you are a believer in Jesus Christ, you will be with the Lord in a world that has no end. You are not and never will be alone without hope, without joy, without life.

God keeps His promises for millennia. He is still keeping a vow He made to Noah that He would never again destroy the earth with a flood. He remains faithful to the pledge He made to Abram thousands of years ago that He would bless all the nations through Abram's seed, who is Jesus, the son of Abraham, the Promised One, our Savior and Redeemer. He announced that He would establish for King David a dynasty of kings who would perpetually reign. Jesus is the final king in that royal order, and He reigns and will reign, with His Father, forevermore.

God tells the truth. He keeps His promises, forever and ever, never ceasing, time without end.

God's Peace Is Perfect

This treatise concerning God's perfection is not simply an exercise in theology. It has real-world consequences. God's unerring knowledge of future events should give us peace in stressful situations. Perhaps this analogy will prove helpful. If you watch a football game on delayed broadcast and know your team has already won, you are not anxious about the outcome, even though as you watch, you see that your team is behind in the final minutes of the fourth quarter. In a sense, you have perfect sovereign knowledge of that small bit of information. If we are sons and daughters of our amazing Father, we have access to the peace of the One who knows all things at all times. If we earnestly strive to keep our minds steadfast on this perfect-knowledge-of-the-end-from-the-beginning

God, there is peace there, perfect peace.[21] He knows the outcome of "your game," so to speak—He has known it since the beginning of time.

However, one may ask, what if the outcome of my game is not good?

God's Love and Goodness Are Perfect

The outcome, the end, of all those who believe in Jesus Christ will be good because God is trustworthy and upright. He knows all things, can do all things, is meticulously aware of all that we need, and possesses the ability to supply it. For those who love Him, He is able to make everything work for good.[22] He has provided and will provide "all things that pertain to life and godliness."[23] Nothing has been or will be excluded. Such exclusion is not possible for the One whose knowledge and power are infallible; whose love and reliability are complete, without error, for eternity.

God is not in a muddle of moral conundrums. It is impossible that He does not know and understand what is beneficial and necessary concerning your circumstances, and thus somehow not know what is eternally life-giving in it all. The Lord Almighty is the referent for what is right and righteous. He created the concept of good as we know it. All that is noble and excellent has God as its origin. He is, in truth, the only One who knows what good is, in the ultimate, enduring sense of things. There is no evil intent or betrayal whatsoever in the heart of God, only loyalty and steadfastness. He is holy: morally pure and spotless, caring and kind. No darkness dwells in Him, He who is the light of the world. He does not submit to wickedness, treachery, or perversion. He lives only in purity. He grasps no selfishness and displays no arrogance. The outcome of your "game" will be good; otherwise, God is not good, and God is not God.

---

21. Isaiah 26:3.
22. Romans 8:28.
23. 2 Peter 1:3.

The Revealing of God's Perfect Work

Jeremiah, in spite of his suffering, wrote, "The LORD is good to those who wait for him, to the soul who seeks him."[24] This verse tells us that if a person seeks and waits for the Lord, he or she will eventually understand that He is good. Those who have become embittered against God may have exalted their pain and doubt above the possibility of knowing this robust truth. However, He understands this and is compassionate when we doubt. Christians who come through excruciating experiences still believing in God's tireless and tender kindness are those who have sought and waited for Him to be known as the God who is good. We are confronted with this truth. We must either believe it or reject it. The thought that God is unwavering in His benevolence may be astounding, but, if believed, is comforting. We fallen sinners are all too aware of the many things that are stupefyingly wrong on the earth in order for this truth to be swallowed easily. Yet, we must eat of it. It may be bitter in our mouths, but it will be sweet to our stomachs. We will not understand the perfection of His will and love until we are with Him. At that time, all secrets will be made known.

Critics of Christianity may claim that God's work is not good, but rather, phenomenally tragic. However, they are not qualified to be His judges. They do not know nor have they experienced the nature of eternity. They are unable to determine, from an eternal perspective, if the Lord is a consummately just and blameless God. In fact, they do not possess a criterion for perfection, because they themselves are not perfect. Therefore, human beings do not have the capacity to judge God's work because they cannot see the end of all things. Only the Christian God makes that claim; therefore, He alone is the indisputable good and just Actor in the fabric of human history.

What is good in any circumstance we find ourselves facing? He is. What does this mean, in a practical sense? Not much and everything. Not much in the sense that believing He has your ultimate good at heart does not cause the difficult, even terrifying

---

24. Lamentations 3:25.

situation to blow away like thistledown in the wind. These trials are exhaustingly, perhaps grievously, weathered in faith. We may think James unfeeling when he wrote, "Is anyone among you suffering? Let him pray,"[25] but we know in our hearts that this is the crux of the matter for us. Yes, it is helpful to have other believers come alongside to pray, strengthen, and encourage, but when all is said and done, when everyone is gone and the lights turned down, one must face the questions, the doubts, the fears, alone with God. No quick and easy answers exist that solve these issues in an immediate way. However, when one answers "amen" to the certainty of God's goodness what is immediate and seemingly interminable fades in the light of eternal reality and truth. Yes, they fade even in death, which we in the Western culture regard as the ultimately bad outcome. However, death is not the ultimately bad outcome. Not knowing the Father and the Lord Jesus is. Death comes to us all. It always has, and it always will, until the Lord Jesus returns. However, Jesus, the slain and risen God-in-the-flesh, conquered death—forever.

Jesus, the Perfect Sacrifice

Jesus, innocent, took the blame for the sins of everyone in the world. Jesus suffered a terrible death because we have sinned. He never did.[26] It is imperative that Jesus was clean and pure because if there was imperfection in Him, any fault whatsoever, it would then be possible that some sinfulness was not covered in His sacrifice. Though guiltless, He absorbed all of the punishment—the fathomless, soul-battering concussion of it—for all people, for all time. If we are in Him, He will take us to where He is. He promised.

And God always keeps His promises.

Always.

---

25. James 5:13a.
26. 1 Peter 1:19.

The God We Do Not Know

Our Glorious Place of Residence

Our ultimate good resides in the glorious place to which the apostle John was taken up, described in Revelation 22:1–5: "Then the angel showed me the river of the water of life, bright as crystal, flowing from the throne of God and of the Lamb through the middle of the street of the city; also, on either side of the river, the tree of life with its twelve kinds of fruit, yielding its fruit each month. The leaves of the tree were for the healing of the nations. No longer will there be anything accursed, but the throne of God and of the Lamb will be in it, and his servants will worship him. They will see his face, and his name will be on their foreheads. And night will be no more. They will need no light of lamp or sun, for the Lord God will be their light, and they will reign forever and ever."

This is the magnificent residence that you and I will one day inhabit, if we believe in and hold fast to Jesus. This home will be perfect, and we will dwell with a perfectly good, supremely powerful, limitless, creative God, our loving Father, and our Savior, Jesus, whose nature will never change.[27]

Knowing by faith this to be the truth, believers endeavor, by God's grace, to adopt an eternal perspective. What we face today, as horrendous or wonderful as it may be, cannot be compared to the glory that will be revealed and will continue to be revealed, for ten thousand times ten thousand millennia and more. Since this is the eternal truth, we join our voices with those in heaven and on the earth, proclaiming with unequaled fervor, "After this I looked, and behold, a great multitude that no one could number, from every nation, from all tribes and peoples and languages, standing before the throne and before the Lamb, clothed in white robes, with palm branches in their hands, and crying out with a loud voice, 'Salvation belongs to our God who sits on the throne, and to the Lamb!' And all the angels were standing around the throne and around the elders and the four living creatures, and they fell on their faces before the throne and worshiped God, saying, 'Amen!

---

27. Malachi 3:6.

Blessing and glory and wisdom and thanksgiving and honor and power and might be to our God forever and ever! Amen.'"[28]

---

28. Revelation 7:9–12.

In order to become like children, Jesus is instructing us that we must turn and humble ourselves.

From What Should We Turn?

What is it that Jesus is telling us to turn away from? It seems clear He is saying that we must turn from the kind of thinking that His disciples had exhibited when they asked, "Who is the greatest in the kingdom of heaven?" In fact, Jesus made that obvious when He stated, "Whoever humbles himself like this child is the greatest in the kingdom of heaven." The childlike trait that Jesus emphasizes here is humility in opposition to greatness, so called. However, this does not fully solve our problem of understanding what Jesus meant. How does one humble oneself like a child? How are children humble? Biblical scholar Ulrich Luz summed it up well in his commentary on Matthew:

> It is important to remember here the negative social situation of children in antiquity. Children were not full human beings with their own integrity but incomplete (νήπιοι, *beings ranging from fetal status to puberty*[3]) beings who needed to be trained; that is, they were not yet grown. Judaism often regarded them negatively as beings not yet capable of making judgments. "Morning sleep and midday wine and children's talk and sitting in the meeting houses of the ignorant people put a man out of the world" (m. 'Abot 3.11).[4] That, as is well known, the words παῖς (*child*[5]) and παιδίον (*very young child*[6]) can also mean "slave," says a great deal about the legal standing of children, who were subject to the unlimited

---

3. Bauer, *Greek-English Lexicon*, 671 s.v. νήπιοι. (Greek literature definition added.)

4. Cf. the triad often appearing in Jewish texts: "deaf mutes, feeble minded, children" (*m. Erub.* 3.2; *m. B. Qam.* 4.4; 6.2, 4); "women, slaves, children" (*m. Šeqal.* 1.3; *m. Sukk.* 2.8; 3.10). (Original note.)

5. Bauer, *Greek-English Lexicon*, 750 s.v. παῖς. (Definition added.)

6. Ibid., 748 s.v. παιδίον. (Definition added.)

The God Who Is Like a Child

authority of their fathers.[7] The point of comparison for our logion is thus first of all children's physical size, then also their powerlessness and their low social standing. Disciples who are like children are thus small, insignificant, and without power.[8]

Jesus is informing us that we must turn from the human thinking that sets greatness as one of the mileposts on the road to significance and fulfillment. Instead of that worldly mindset, we must humble ourselves like powerless children.

The Nature of God's Kingdom

According to Jesus, being great in His kingdom equals becoming deliberately small and without power, even like a slave, in contrast to the influence and supremacy His disciples craved and which the world esteems so highly. It would require impotence in a world that lusts for dominance. This is the humility of a child to which Jesus refers. Children have authority over very little, and in the adult world, they have no authority whatsoever. Adolescents do not successfully run corporations or governments. By virtue of inheritance, they may receive money or a royal position, but they do not possess the maturity to manage them. To wield effective, significant power, they must reach the age of majority.

This is Jesus, again, profoundly contrasting our understanding of how His kingdom functions with the custom and practice of the world. It is not necessary to go into a lengthy investigation of how greatness is perceived in all cultures. We all know how the world operates, effectively gets things done, and what it values, whether it is in the realm of government, business, or tribe. It would not be inaccurate to say that what is prized among all these realms are power, money, influence, status, or some combination thereof. Therefore, our great conundrum, our immense

---

7. Unlike τέκνον that underscores the relationship of the child to its parents. (Original note.)
8. Luz, *Matthew 8-20*, 428–29.

struggle, is to discover how in the world Christians are to function or even exist in this kind of world if they are to become as small and powerless as children. It is momentously important that we enter this struggle, because Jesus said that we can never enter His kingdom unless we do. The acknowledgement that we wrestle so greatly with a real-world answer to this question should indicate to us how little we know about our God.

In the verses concerning childlikeness we read earlier, we find a jolting counterintuitive meaning of the nature of His dominion. Followers of Jesus Christ are not to rule at all in God's kingdom on earth. Just the opposite. If they do not become like powerless children, they are not even in the kingdom—*never* will be, in fact. This is a disorienting truth. Jesus has tossed another spiritual grenade right into the middle of our hierarchical religious world.

I am not sure whether I should laugh at His amazing, controversial words or crawl into a fetal position when I consider the reality of following them. Are you looking for an easy answer? I have none. What Jesus teaches in Matthew 18:1–4 takes all of our preconceived, inherited understanding of earthly power and greatness, rolls it into a ball, and throws it against the walls of the Church to be irreparably broken—which is what we should expect from the God we do not know.

The Knowledge of Jesus Versus Mighty Works

The verses below trouble me. The people Jesus warns us about were, according to their perception, doing mighty works, but they were unknown to Him. Is it possible to value the greatness that accompanies significant ministry more than a seemingly powerless, childlike knowledge of Jesus and His kingdom? That is a very real possibility. "Not everyone who says to me, 'Lord, Lord,' will enter the kingdom of heaven, but the one who does the will of my Father who is in heaven. On that day many will say to me, 'Lord, Lord, did we not prophesy in your name, and cast out demons in your name, and do many mighty works in your name?' And then will I declare to them, 'I never knew you; depart from me, you workers of lawlessness.'"[9]

When Jesus cast from His presence those who had done significant works but did not know Him, He made it clear that a living, obedient relationship with the Lord and entering His kingdom is vastly more important than noteworthy accomplishments performed in His name. The unfortunate individuals who were cast from Jesus' presence had acquired a tragic misconception about what is essentially important about the kingdom of God.

The Wondrous God Who Is Like a Child

However, the dismantling of our understanding of prominence in God's kingdom is not the only stunning implication of Jesus' teaching in Matthew 18. Let's look at verse 4 again: "Whoever humbles himself like this child is the greatest in the kingdom of heaven." Is Jesus telling us that if we humble ourselves that we will be the greatest in the kingdom of heaven?

Perhaps the answer can be found by asking another question. Is Jesus Himself in the kingdom of heaven? Of course He is. He is indisputably the greatest in the kingdom of heaven. There is none greater. Therefore, Jesus, remarkably, is telling us that He humbled Himself like a child. How was Jesus like a child? He was like a child because in His incarnation, He became profoundly powerless. He had enjoyed unlimited dominion in heaven. Indeed, Scripture tells us that "All things were made through him, and without him was not any thing made that was made."[10] This is an astonishing truth claim about the unlimited might of God. When we study the universe, the earth, and the flora and fauna that exist on it, we continue to discover wonders that boggle the minds of scientists. Jesus, with His Father and the Holy Spirit, conceptualized from nothing all that we study and spoke it all into existence. Similarly,

---

9. Matthew 7:21–23.
10. John 1:3.

we are told that Jesus is "the radiance of the glory of God and the exact imprint of his nature, and he upholds the universe by the word of his power."[11]

How He does this upholding is unknown to us. When I read the bewildering, unlike-the-real-world facts about quantum mechanics, I wonder with joy if physicists are studying the word of His power at work.

Since we are so overwhelmed with astonishment by the nature of God's power in creation, it is no surprise how difficult it is for us to comprehend the omnipotence and glory Jesus relinquished when He left heaven. No abdication of earthly power or status will ever offer an appropriate analogy, because not one of us is God. The Lord is the most supreme, awe-inspiring Being that is possible for us to know. We may be humbled by a reduction or loss of status, position, money, or influence, but these pale in comparison—no, they offer no comparison at all—to the diminishment Jesus experienced when He left heaven to become God incarnate in the body of a man.

We have heard so much about Jesus' birth in a stable that it almost ceases to have meaning to us anymore. Nevertheless, let's think about the reality of this event. The power-over-everything King of the universe showed up on earth as a helpless baby. Perhaps we could imagine such a thing. However, this baby would grow up to become a Superman, a Wolverine, an Ironman; an individual who, by his physical, other-worldly, or man-made strength, would defeat evil and the bad guys. However, Paul tells us in Philippians that Jesus "emptied himself" when He walked among us.[12] Yes, He demonstrated by His Spirit power over nature, demons, and sickness, but He did not usurp control of any earthly power or organization. He could have gathered to Himself all the wealth and might of the world with just a word in order to support Himself, His followers, or His ministry. Instead, He remained poor. He could have taken immediate charge over all the lawlessness and injustice in the earth, but He did not. If He had annihilated on the spot all

---

11. Hebrews 1:3a.
12. Philippians 2:7.

those who were trying to murder Him, we would understand. It would have made sense to us. That is how superior power works. He did not become an all-world king or earthly deliverer, the powers with which Satan tempted Him, nor did He exercise authority over people and demand they do His bidding. In comparison to the power He could have wielded; in comparison to the supremacy He once possessed in heaven, He became as a relatively powerless child and laid aside His right to primacy: He "did not count equality with God a thing to be grasped."[13] He became so powerless that He "humbled himself by becoming obedient to the point of death, even death on a cross."[14] This is the ultimate, enfeebled humility: the physical death of God Himself. Yet, out of this self-imposed degradation emerged the strongest victory possible: the eternal destruction of death, hell, sin, the grave, and the devil.

Who humbled himself like an insignificant child? Jesus did. Who is the greatest in the kingdom of heaven? He is. The One who humbled Himself the most has become the greatest in the kingdom of heaven. "Therefore God has highly exalted him and bestowed on him the name that is above every name, so that at the name of Jesus every knee should bow, in heaven and on earth and under the earth, and every tongue confess that Jesus Christ is Lord, to the glory of God the Father."[15]

Jesus' Childlikeness Burns Down Our Religious Reality

Jesus would not command us to do what He Himself did not. If He took upon Himself the tattered rags of earthly impotence, what should we do? This is the undeniable, house-burning-down reality of childlikeness that Jesus proffers. We can ignore it. We can whistle our way past it. We can allow our eyes to glaze over as we read Matthew 18:1–4. However, the price of that ignorance is

---

13. Philippians 2:6b.
14. Philippians 2:8b.
15. Philippians 2:9–11.

costly: We will never enter God's kingdom. If you are a sincere Christian, it is obvious that entering His kingdom is your desire, since Jesus told us to seek that kingdom.[16]

Do I have advice to offer about how to become a powerless child and thus enter His kingdom? No, not a three-point, five-point, or twenty-point strategy, only this: We must know Him. We must study how He led and lived. We must lay that mind-bending warning He spoke in Matthew 18 before Him and pray, "I hacve only a small notion of how to do what You command. Please help me become like a child. I want to enter Your kingdom." Now we have humbled ourselves, another step in our quest to know Him. He will answer this prayer. How can I say this with such assurance? Because we are praying this in our endeavor to listen to His words and obey them, both of which are His will. It will be difficult to journey down this path. However, He is gracious. He compassionately understands that He is the God we do not know.

---

16. Matthew 6:33.

6

The Unexpected God

For my thoughts are not your thoughts,
neither are your ways my ways, declares the LORD.[1]

～ The Lord to Israel

MY MOTHER DIED OF colon cancer when I was sixteen. When I visited her in the hospital—times all too few, as I reflect back—I beheld a skeleton, skin stretched over bone. What I experienced in her room—the smells, the sterile starchiness of the place—remain with me today, a profoundly sad and dreadful memory. After her death, when I walked around the house, I often saw things that reminded me of her. One afternoon, I opened a drawer and found her make-up compact. I broke down and wept. At her funeral, I cried and cried until no tears remained. I was so devastated that everything, including food, became unimportant. Even though her passing is decades past, it is not unusual for me, even now, to get choked up when I speak of her. No one in the family, least of all me, expected her to die this way. To my adolescent mind, it seemed that she was gone much too quickly and much too soon. Although I was already a lost and rebellious youth, I soon embarked upon a self-destructive path of risky alcohol and drug abuse. However,

1. Isaiah 55:8.

five years after my mom's death, God mercifully intervened. I became a Christian. I sometimes wonder if the prayers of a dying woman had anything to do with the salvation of a very wayward young man.

More good news was yet to come. Four years after my conversion, I attended our denomination's international convention for the first time. One of the seminars addressed the topic of church administration. Around thirty of us were present in a small classroom that morning. The teacher had started his instruction, and I was drinking foul-tasting coffee from a Styrofoam cup. Suddenly, a thought went through my mind, completely out of context, having no relevance whatsoever to the subject matter at hand: *You are going to be the pastor of a church in Wilbur, Washington.* This was a completely unexpected idea. I hadn't considered that position for myself at all. I was working as an office assistant for a church in Spokane, Washington—that's why I was in the seminar. In fact, there was no church of our denominational stripe in that place, only a Bible study. Not only was this an unanticipated thought; it was a life-changing one. When Laurie and I returned home, I told the pastor what I believed the Lord had spoken to me, and within one month we were installed as pastors in that small town. I was a bright and shiny twenty-six-year-old man with no pastoral experience. Many of the congregants were old enough to be our parents.

Unforeseen events occur in all of our lives. Some bring joy; others devastation. We celebrate weddings, new babies, and tax refunds. However, a law enforcement officer at our front door bearing tragic news about a loved one injured in an automobile accident, or a doctor's diagnosis of a spreading, malignant cancer can, in a moment, place us on a road of sadness, confusion, and fear. The trajectory of our lives can change in an instant. No one is immune.

The Unexpected Messiah

Regardless of how we respond to unpredictable circumstances, whether they are accompanied by sadness or joy, the Christian

The Unexpected God

God is the indisputable sovereign Lord of the unexpected, and He often arrives like a life-upending tsunami. If we were to peruse the whole of Scripture, we would discover that God's preference is to perform His will in ways that are quite unimagined by believers and nonbelievers alike. The situations we read about in the Bible may seem quite foreign to us, but the God who is involved with them is not—or shouldn't be. The most obvious example that likely comes to mind of the Lord's unpredictability is Gabriel's announcement to Mary, an unmarried virgin, that she would become pregnant with a child whom she was to call Jesus, the Son of the Most High.[2] This had not happened to any woman in history and will never again. Nevertheless, this was a joyous, though enormously life-altering and potentially humiliating proclamation, clearly unexpected by both Mary and Joseph.

However, another much less pleasing communication occurred around thirty years later, not to Mary, but to her nephew, John the Baptist. Jesus was approached by John's disciples who asked on his behalf, "Are you the one who is to come, or shall we look for another?"[3] Jesus answered John's question with the evidence provided by His ministry: "Go and tell John what you hear and see: the blind receive their sight and the lame walk, lepers are cleansed and the deaf hear, and the dead are raised up, and the poor have good news preached to them. And blessed is the one who is not offended by me."[4]

John, who previously had given witness to the arrival of the Lamb who was to take away the sins of the world,[5] was having second thoughts. Apparently, John was expecting the Messiah to be not only the Sin Bearer, but also the greater David, the one who was to reestablish the kingdom of Israel and restore its golden days. However, Jesus was the unexpected Messiah. Israel's desire centered on a victorious, Maccabean-like warrior. Instead, they were given a suffering servant. Therefore, they did not recognize

2. Luke 1:26–38.
3. Matthew 11:3.
4. Matthew 11:4–6.
5. John 1:29.

Him. The apostle John wrote: "He was in the world, and the world was made through him, yet the world did not know him. He came to his own, and his own people did not receive him."[6]

Jesus' answer to John the Baptist's inquiry confirmed that He was healing people and bringing good news to the poor, but He was not accomplishing anything in the political and military arenas at all.

Jesus was the unexpected Messiah to John the Baptist in yet another way. Jesus' reference in the earlier passage from Matthew that "the poor have the good news preached to them" was from the messianic portion of Isaiah 61. Note that Jesus omitted the last part of the verse in His message to John: "The Spirit of the Lord God is upon me, because the Lord has anointed me to bring good news to the poor; he has sent me to bind up the brokenhearted, to proclaim liberty to the captives, *and the opening of the prison to those who are bound.*"[7]

This omission was Jesus' way of saying, "John, not only am I not going to fulfill the messianic expectations of present-day Israel and thus conquer and expel the Roman occupiers, I am also not going to be the one who releases you from prison." John the Baptist heard the brutal truth of an unanticipated reality: "I will not open the prison doors and set you free." Unexpectedly, Jesus allowed John, the greatest born of women, to suffer decapitation and martyrdom.[8]

His Unexpected Second Coming

Because He is the unexpected God, Christians often miss Him, too. It worries me when Jesus says things like this: "And will not God give justice to his elect, who cry to him day and night? Will he delay long over them? I tell you, he will give justice to them speedily. Nevertheless, when the Son of Man comes, will he find faith on

---

6. John 1:10–11.
7. Isaiah 61:1, italics added.
8. Matthew 11:11; 14:6–12.

earth?"[9] "You also must be ready, for the Son of Man is coming at an hour you do not expect."[10]

These warnings concern me because they include me. My natural tendency is to pass these admonitions off and assume Jesus is talking about someone else. May that not be true of you and me. These verses should engender a potent measure of fear in us because we have managed to miss Him, with few exceptions, every time He or His representatives have shown up in the midst of His people. Consider Noah's flood, the time to which Jesus compared the season of His coming. Jesus said of that event: "For as were the days of Noah, so will be the coming of the Son of Man. For as in those days before the flood they were eating and drinking, marrying and giving in marriage, until the day when Noah entered the ark, and they were unaware until the flood came and swept them all away, so will be the coming of the Son of Man."[11]

It is possible, I suppose, that the inhabitants of that time never questioned why Noah, a herald of righteousness, was building a huge ship that required one hundred years to complete. Perhaps those people were incredibly stupid. However, I doubt it. What is probable is that they simply ignored Noah and continued with the ordinary routine of their lives, which is what Jesus said they did: "in those days before the flood they were eating and drinking, marrying and giving in marriage." Then the Lord brought the "unexpected" judgment. Eating and drinking are normal, every-day activities. Marrying and giving in marriage are biblical commands given for our joy and the continuance of the race. However, these commonplace pursuits were not accompanied by serious attention to the judgment that Noah was announcing. Are Christians in danger of doing the same? Again, Jesus said, "You also must be ready, for the Son of Man is coming at an hour you do not expect."[12]

The truth about His unanticipated return is reiterated in the writings of three different apostles:

9. Luke 18:7–8.
10. Luke 12:40.
11. Matthew 24:37–39.
12. Luke 12:40.

Peter: But the day of the Lord will come like a thief, and then the heavens will pass away with a roar, and the heavenly bodies will be burned up and dissolved, and the earth and the works that are done on it will be exposed (2 Peter 3:10).

John: Behold, I am coming like a thief! Blessed is the one who stays awake, keeping his garments on, that he may not go about naked and be seen exposed! (Revelation 16:15).

Paul: For you yourselves are fully aware that the day of the Lord will come like a thief in the night. While people are saying, "There is peace and security," then sudden destruction will come upon them as labor pains come upon a pregnant woman, and they will not escape. But you are not in darkness, brothers, for that day to surprise you like a thief (1 Thessalonians 5:2-4).

May we, like Paul said of those Thessalonian brothers and sisters, not be surprised by the coming of the Thief. However, we must stay awake, as the Lord counselled. Jesus is the unexpected God.

Unexpected Evangelism

Do you have a preferred method of evangelism? A few of us are street preachers—not many. Some elect to do what is called friendship evangelism. Perhaps most of us choose to leave that work to the pastor when he makes the call for repentance and salvation after a church service. Many others, mostly in "underdeveloped" countries, take advantage of the opportunities to present the gospel that arise when people are healed of physical ailments or delivered from demonic influences. However, no one would ever think of the method that the Lord used in Acts 5. Truly, no one but our sovereign God would ever conceive of such a thing. Here is what the Bible says happened after the Lord took the lives of Ananias and Sapphira for lying about how much they had given to the church: "And great fear came upon the whole church and upon all who heard of these things."[13] The Christians and other local people were afraid. This is perfectly understandable. If you might die because you told a lie to the apostles, that might stimulate a bit of caution. Verse 13 of this same chapter makes sense, too: "None of the rest dared join them, but the people held them in high esteem." Who wouldn't be reluctant to hang around with people who, because you lie to them, cause you to end up dead on the floor, by simply speaking a word? However, it is also a bit counterintuitive, one would think. Something miraculous happens in your ministry and no one wants to join you because of it. Is that the way to grow a church?

Apparently it is, because the real stunner arrives in the next verse: "And more than ever believers were added to the Lord, multitudes of both men and women."[14]

Does this mean that the Lord's killing of two people brought men and women to Him?

It seems that was the case, according to this account.

Who would have ever thought of that method of evangelism?

Only our unexpected God.

Unexpected evangelism occurred at least two more times in the book of Acts. In Acts 16:9, we are told that the Lord gave Paul a vision of a Macedonian man saying, "Come over to Macedonia and help us." Paul and Silas were obedient and departed. However, it was not long after they arrived in the Macedonian city of Philippi that the inhabitants beat Paul and Silas with rods, threw them in jail, and secured their feet in stocks. While they were incarcerated, praying and singing hymns to God, the prison was shaken by an earthquake. All the prison doors were opened, and the bonds of the inmates were unfastened. The jailer wanted to kill himself, since he would be held accountable for the loss of those in his charge, but Paul shouted out that none had escaped. Consequently, the jailer and his family came to know the Lord.[15]

---

13. Acts 5:11.
14. Acts 5:14.
15. Acts 16:16–34.

Bringing an earthquake to the neighborhood is not how we would plan our evangelistic campaigns, even if we could.

The third example of unexpected evangelism is in Acts 19. The infamous seven sons of Sceva were attempting to cast out demons, saying, "I adjure you by the Jesus whom Paul proclaims." However, the evil spirit in the man was not impressed by these words and said, "Jesus I know, and Paul I recognize, but who are you?" The possessed man jumped on those seven men, beat them up, and stripped them of their clothing. The result? "And this became known to all the residents of Ephesus, both Jews and Greeks. And fear fell upon them all, and the name of the Lord Jesus was extolled. Also many of those who were now believers came, confessing and divulging their practices. And a number of those who had practiced magic arts brought their books together and burned them in the sight of all. And they counted the value of them and found it came to fifty thousand pieces of silver. So the word of the Lord continued to increase and prevail mightily."[16]

No one preached. No one presented the gospel at that time. People became believers and repented of their sins. Why? Because some false believers were attempting to delve into a dangerous area of spiritual warfare for which they were tragically unequipped. The demons they endeavored to cast out respected the name of Jesus, the One who had ultimate authority, but not these seven sons who were subsequently beaten and humiliated. We could not possibly plan such an event for the purpose of evangelism, and there is little doubt that we would have anticipated a positive outcome even if we had.

However, our God is Lord of all. He does whatever He pleases[17]—often unexpectedly, and always for His glory, not ours.

---

16. Acts 19:13b, 15–20.
17. Psalm 115:3.

The Unexpected Call

The Lord God calls individuals into His service after the counsel of His own will. He does not send a polite "You are invited" note before His summons arrives. He just simply calls, and His call is irresistible. Oh, I suppose one could resist, as Jonah did, but we know how that turned out for the reluctant prophet. We are also aware of the result of Jeremiah's attempt to reject God's call to prophesy to the nations. Jeremiah informed the Lord that he was too young for such a task. This was the Lord's response to his complaint: "Do not say, 'I am only a youth'; for to all to whom I send you, you shall go, and whatever I command you, you shall speak. Do not be afraid of them, for I am with you to deliver you, declares the Lord."[18]

That settled the matter, apparently.

Moses was at work as a shepherd when the Lord called him by means of a burning bush in the wilderness.[19] Moses was a murderer, an outcast from his own people for forty years. He was an unlikely candidate to be the man who would confront Pharaoh on behalf of God's people. Therefore, perhaps it should not surprise us that Moses attempted to reject God's call by endeavoring to educate the Lord about his insufficient oratory talent.[20] Nevertheless, Moses did not win this argument. It ended like this: "You shall speak all that I command you, and your brother Aaron shall tell Pharaoh to let the people of Israel go out of his land."[21]

Resistance is . . . ineffective.

And God's call unexpected.

The Lord's call to young Samuel to prophesy to Eli was so unanticipated that the lad thought he was being summoned by the priest.[22]

---

18. Jeremiah 1:7–8.
19. Exodus 3:1–4.
20. Exodus 6:12, 30.
21. Exodus 7:2.
22. 1 Samuel 3:1–14.

David, like Moses, was also out by himself with the sheep when he was summoned by Samuel to be anointed king.[23] He was not the eldest son and the first born. He was the youngest and the last. This was not how the good prophet Samuel thought the leader of God's people would be chosen. "When they came, he looked on Eliab and thought, 'Surely the Lord's anointed is before him.' But the Lord said to Samuel, 'Do not look on his appearance or on the height of his stature, because I have rejected him. For the Lord sees not as man sees: man looks on the outward appearance, but the Lord looks on the heart.'"[24]

One might conclude from these accounts that a person needs to be alone, quiet, and away from people in order to hear the Lord's unlooked-for call. This is untrue.

James and John were mending nets with their father when Jesus beckoned them to follow.[25]

Matthew was at work collecting taxes.[26]

Zacchaeus, also a tax collector, was called out by Jesus in a public place after he had climbed a tree in order to see Him better.[27]

Paul was traveling with a group of men on their way to persecute Christians when the Lord confronted and called him.[28]

It would not be possible to include here the innumerable accounts of individuals in the history of the Church who have heard or experienced the unforeseen call from the Lord, either to salvation or service. At this present time in history, there are reports of people from the Middle East who have never had the opportunity to hear the Gospel or read the Bible, whom the Lord is calling to Himself via dreams and visions. In this, we greatly rejoice.

---

23. 1 Samuel 16:11–12.
24. 1 Samuel 16:6–7.
25. Matthew 4:21–22.
26. Matthew 9:9.
27. Luke 19:1–10.
28. Acts 9:1–8.

How About You?

Has the Lord God arrived on your doorstep unannounced? Has His arrival brought good news, warning, or both? Has He called you to Himself? If not, I encourage you to seek Him. He is the unexpected God, but He is not a God who cannot be discovered and known. "You will seek me and find me, when you seek me with all your heart."[29] If you ask and keep asking, He will be found. However, He is likely to arrive when He is least expected. At that time, worship Him and be exceedingly glad. You have been visited by the God you will now be endeavoring to know.

---

29. Jeremiah 29:13.

7

The God Who Is Gentle and Lowly in Heart

Take my yoke upon you, and learn from me,
for I am gentle and lowly in heart,
and you will find rest for your souls.[1]

~ Jesus

OUR GOD IS ALIVE with wonder, a soul-filling conflagration of improbable truth. He loves us as He detonates our spiritual assumptions, turning our religious worlds upside down.

This is the God of the Bible. This is our Savior, Jesus.

We see Him in Scripture, the writers using words rich with magnificence to describe the Lord of all that exists. The passage that follows, in which John attempted to set forth the heavenly scene he was witnessing, is an overwhelming example of the wonder of our glorious Lord: "At once I was in the Spirit, and behold, a throne stood in heaven, with one seated on the throne. And he who sat there had the appearance of jasper and carnelian, and around the throne was a rainbow that had the appearance of an emerald. Around the throne were twenty-four thrones, and seated on the thrones were twenty-four elders, clothed in white garments,

---

1. Matthew 11:29.

The God Who Is Gentle and Lowly in Heart

with golden crowns on their heads. From the throne came flashes of lightning, and rumblings and peals of thunder, and before the throne were burning seven torches of fire, which are the seven spirits of God."[2]

The sovereign Lord appeared to be made of shaped, precious stone. Lightning flashed, and thunder boomed from His throne. Blazing torches burned before Him. Crowned elders encircled Him, themselves enthroned. God's seat of rulership is a joyously powerful, fear-inducing, turbulent place. Amazing stuff, and I am sure we all agree that human words will always be insufficient to describe our remarkable God. We shouldn't be surprised, should we? He is the one true God, the Lord God of the universe, and we are hard put to express His greatness.

In spite of our incompetence at describing the Creator of all things, I would like to reflect on two of His characteristics that we do not often consider, words which seem quite incompatible with the depiction we just read, although they were used by Jesus to describe Himself in Matthew 11:29: He is gentle and lowly in heart. Gentle and lowly *in heart* would indicate that this attribute is at the core of His being.

Is this the God we know? One who is gentle and lowly in heart?

The Mighty God Was Rejected by the Wise and Intelligent

Let's back up a bit to understand the context in which Jesus makes this astonishing claim about Himself. He had just rebuked the people who lived in the cities of Chorazin, Bethsaida, and Capernaum: "Woe to you, Chorazin! Woe to you, Bethsaida! For if the mighty works done in you had been done in Tyre and Sidon, they would have repented long ago in sackcloth and ashes. But I tell you, it will be more bearable on the day of judgment for Tyre and Sidon than for you. And you, Capernaum, will you be exalted to heaven? You

---

2. Revelation 4:2–5.

will be brought down to Hades. For if the mighty works done in you had been done in Sodom, it would have remained until this day. But I tell you that it will be more tolerable on the day of judgment for the land of Sodom than for you."[3]

Although Jesus had done mighty works in those three cities, they had not repented and turned to God. He told the inhabitants of Chorazin and Bethsaida that if such miracles had been performed in the proud and sinful cities of Tyre and Sidon, they would have repented in sackcloth and ashes. Jesus' last devastating hammer stroke to the citizenry of those areas was that it will be more tolerable on the Day of Judgment for Tyre and Sidon than for them. Jesus then announced to Capernaum that if the mighty works they had witnessed had been done in Sodom, upon which He hurled sulfur and fire, it would not have been destroyed. That is a jaw-dropping condemnation. To be compared to the evil city of Sodom is quite a rebuke, but Jesus delivered it because He knew how important it was for His people to acknowledge Him as the Messiah. It is clear that He expected them to believe in Him because of the wondrous works He had done. He proclaimed this truth in John 5:36, as well: "But the testimony that I have is greater than that of John. For the works that the Father has given me to accomplish, the very works that I am doing, bear witness about me that the Father has sent me."

Jesus expected the people of Israel to understand that He was the one spoken of in the book of Isaiah, which He quoted when He stood up to read in the synagogue at Nazareth at the beginning of His ministry: "The Spirit of the Lord is upon me, because he has anointed me to proclaim good news to the poor. He has sent me to proclaim liberty to the captives and recovering of sight to the blind, to set at liberty those who are oppressed, to proclaim the year of the Lord's favor."[4]

However, the prophecies from Isaiah, other prophets, and the miracles were not enough, apparently. These leaders were so unconvinced by Jesus' wondrous works that they claimed instead

---

3. Matthew 11:21–24.
4. Luke 4:18–19.

that He was casting out demons by the prince of demons, not the power of God.[5]

So, why had these cities rejected Him, in spite of the miracles He performed? He was so unlike the Messiah they anticipated that they could not comprehend, by their human intelligence and learning, how Jesus could be the Expected One. They were anticipating one kind of Messiah, and He was quite another.

The Father's Truth Revealed to Children

After His denunciation of the three cities, Jesus rejoiced before His Father and said, "I thank you, Father, Lord of heaven and earth, that you have hidden these things from the wise and understanding and revealed them to little children; yes, Father, for such was your gracious will."[6]

These little children—Jesus' disciples—were relatively ignorant individuals, without status in the religious community. The scholarly scribes and Pharisees, however, expected God to choose learned and devoutly trained men to do His work. Revealing His nature and ways to an educationally deficient rabble was not how they expected a wise God to behave.[7]

Nevertheless, this revealing of the Father to little children, Jesus says, is the Father's "gracious will." Please allow me to reiterate. It is the Father's will—not only His will, but His *gracious* will—to reveal Himself, not to the wise and intelligent, but to those who are like children. As Leon Morris wrote, "We are not to think that some people of little ability chanced to hit on the truth while more able and profound people missed the mark, and that God then accepted what happened. Jesus is saying that the Father planned things this way."[8]

---

5. Matthew 12:24.
6. Matthew 11:25–26.
7. Acts 4:13
8. Morris, *Gospel According to Matthew*, 293.

Taking Jesus' Yoke

After this rebuke and gracious, counter-intuitive, hostile-to-human-intelligence teaching, Jesus said, "Come to me, all who labor and are heavy laden, and I will give you rest. Take my yoke upon you, and learn from me, for I am gentle and lowly in heart, and you will find rest for your souls. For my yoke is easy, and my burden is light."[9]

Although Jesus exhorted His followers to take His yoke upon them, the Jews of Jesus' time were taught to take upon themselves the yoke of the Torah, as well as the written and oral teachings and traditions, while under the tutelage of rabbis. Jesus was confronting God's people with a staggering contrast of choices: Him or their understanding of their holy books, the authority of the rabbis, and their centuries-long traditions.

Knowledge of God's Word Alone Is Not Enough

The Pharisees knew the written and oral law thoroughly. They memorized it. However, they did not recognize Jesus. He did not meet their expectations of what the Messiah should be. What kind of deliverer did they anticipate? Succinctly stated, they longed for a man who would lead Israel to be a great nation upon the earth.[10] This means that they also anticipated a prophet who would be righteous, a legalistically perfect man: "And he will be clean from sin, to rule over a great people, to reprove rulers, and to remove sinners by the strength of his word. And he will not be weak in his days upon his God, because God made him strong by the Holy Spirit and wise by the counsel of understanding, with strength and righteousness."[11]

---

9. Matthew 11:28–30.

10. Zechariah 8:22–23; Isaiah 11:9–10.

11. Brannan et al., *Lexham English Septuagint,* Psalms of Solomon 17:41–42.

However, according to their understanding, Jesus was a "glutton and a drunkard"[12] and therefore did not fulfill their messianic hopes. They conveniently ignored not only His miraculous works, but many scriptural truths such as Isaiah 53, which includes these precious verses about our lowly Messiah: "He was despised and rejected by men; a man of sorrows, and acquainted with grief; and as one from whom men hide their faces he was despised, and we esteemed him not. Surely he has borne our griefs and carried our sorrows; yet we esteemed him stricken, smitten by God, and afflicted. But he was pierced for our transgressions; he was crushed for our iniquities; upon him was the chastisement that brought us peace, and with his wounds we are healed. All we like sheep have gone astray; we have turned—every one—to his own way; and the Lord has laid on him the iniquity of us all."[13]

Those who consider themselves wise, Jesus said, fail to see God because they think He can be accessed via their selective understanding of Scripture and tradition alone. This perception depends upon one's wisdom and intellect and therefore the interpretation of who they understand God is, what He requires, and what He will do. However, Jesus said they were to learn who the Father was from *Him*: "Take My yoke and learn of *Me*." The laboring, weary, and burdened people Jesus cried out to in these verses were those who had tried by virtue of their intellect and the thinking of man—like the inhabitants of those three cities who thought they were wise possessors of religious knowledge—to find an understanding of God according to law and tradition. Jesus wanted them—and wants us—to be relieved of this burden. He stated plainly that if we came to Him, He would give us rest.

The answer to finding life in God is to know Him, His grace, and be discipled by Jesus like humble children who are willing to admit that they know little or nothing. The answer is to take His yoke, to come under the authority of the One who is low and humble in heart. *He* is the way to the knowledge of God. He *is* knowledge—perfect knowledge. If we don't know how to proceed in our

---

12. Matthew 11:19.
13. Isaiah 53:3–6.

lives under His rulership, the answer is found both by humbly seeking Him and the truths about Him in His Word—not by placing a yoke that requires legalistic adherence to Scripture and tradition, based upon tragically inadequate human comprehension.

The Lethal Result of Human Wisdom and Intelligence

The way to know our humble-in-heart God is not found in the power of our human knowledge alone. We must be careful. We can, with one simple step, move from our ultimate goal of knowing Jesus to imposing *requirements* to know Him, activities which make good sense to our human intelligence. The final results of those endeavors are pride and wearying religious legalism, both of which lead to spiritual decline and danger. We are to encourage and admonish one another to keep under Jesus' yoke, not impose a yoke of any other kind. If we Christians do not exercise great caution, it is quite possible that we will come under this scathing rebuke from Jesus, quoting Isaiah: "You hypocrites! Well did Isaiah prophesy of you, when he said: 'This people honors me with their lips, but their heart is far from me; in vain do they worship me, teaching as doctrines the commandments of men.'"[14]

In such a prideful state, we begin to question the quality of other believers' spiritual lives. "How am I able to know the Lord and what the church expects, and this person isn't? Why is he so ignorant about the right way to do things and the requirements of church membership? Didn't he listen to the pastor's sermon?" This puts us into the category of those whom Jesus called the "wise and prudent," those who think they have this knowing-and-serving-God thing figured out because they have adequately absorbed the biblical admonitions and the traditions of men. This way of thinking is the antithesis of being like a relatively uneducated child and puts us in the group of people to whom the Father graciously chooses *not* to reveal Himself. It results in, surprisingly,

---

14. Matthew 15:7–9.

an inadequacy of the true knowledge of God. We become like the inhabitants of Chorazin, Bethsaida, and Capernaum. No promising future lies ahead for that community. It is a community in bondage—self-righteous and fatigued by a lifetime of activities and beliefs that consume life.

Jesus is low and humble in heart, and when Christian believers take His yoke, it is quite different from the yoke that carries with it the burden of being able to sort it all out and nail it down. The Lord is gracious and compassionate. He understands what we, unbelievably, seem to find so hard to admit: We just do not—will not—cannot—know Him by relying on our wisdom and intelligence. We can strictly follow church traditions and not learn of the living Jesus. We can memorize His Word, parse it, outline it, systematize it—and still not know Him. Oh, yes, the truth is undeniably there, just as it was for the inhabitants of Chorazin, Bethsaida, and Capernaum. It was available to the Pharisees, as well. However, almost all of them missed Him. The disciples failed to see Him, too. However, those twelve, among others, were willing, or, perhaps better said, enabled by faith, to follow Him like children—and humble enough to know that they didn't know.

The Yoke of Jesus Is Kind and Good

We have just seen that Jesus tells us to take His yoke because He is gentle and lowly in heart. However, perhaps we could ask another question: What does it mean that Jesus' yoke is easy and His burden is light? Let's look at the last two verses again in Matthew 11:29–30: "Take my yoke upon you, and learn from me, for I am gentle and lowly in heart, and you will find rest for your souls. For my yoke is easy, and my burden is light." We are commanded to take Jesus' yoke *because* His yoke is easy and His burden light. The Greek word *"chrēstos"* is translated "easy" here. However, this is the only place in the New Testament where it is interpreted this way. It is rendered "good" in these four verses:

- Luke 5:39: And no one after drinking old wine desires new, for he says, "The old is good."
- First Peter 2:3: . . . if indeed you have tasted that the Lord is good.
- Luke 6:35: But love your enemies, and do good, and lend, expecting nothing in return, and your reward will be great, and you will be sons of the Most High, for he is kind to the ungrateful and the evil.
- First Corinthians 15:33: Do not be deceived: "Bad company ruins good morals."

Chrēstos is translated "kind" or "kindness" in the following two verses:

- Ephesians 4:32: Be kind to one another, tenderhearted, forgiving one another, as God in Christ forgave you.
- Romans 2:4: Or do you presume on the riches of his kindness and forbearance and patience, not knowing that God's kindness is meant to lead you to repentance?

Therefore, it is proper to say that Jesus' yoke is "kind and good." The word "easy" may give us the false idea that somehow following Jesus is easy. Indisputably, it is not. We are required to give up our very lives for His sake.[15]

The yoke of Jesus is good. It is good because He is good. He wants what is best for us, both here and in His heavenly kingdom, where our eternal hope and habitation reside. We have the unbelievable privilege of knowing and being the children of the great Creator and sovereign God of the universe. He died in order to provide all this for us. Jesus is good, and His yoke is good in the highest manifestation of that word "good."

The burden of Jesus is light. It is light because it functions in the context of a relationship with Him, the God of grace, and not in a burdensome, legalistic, have-I-done-it-all right yoke of fear. This yoke leads to despair and uncertainty. It is heavy. It weighs

---

15. Luke 14:25–33.

us down with a constellation of rules and regulations that perhaps we have not fulfilled, with the possibility of more to fulfill in the future.

The Low and Gentle Servility of Jesus

Yet, questions remain. Why would Jesus tell us to take His yoke *because* He is gentle and lowly in heart?

A Greek-English Lexicon of the New Testament and Other Early Christian Literature, gives this definition of "gentle": "pertains to not being overly impressed by a sense of one's self-importance, gentle, humble, considerate, meek."[16]

It offers these three definitions of "lowly":

1. pertains to being of low social status or to relative inability to cope, lowly, undistinguished, of no account;
2. pertains to being servile in manner, pliant, subservient, abject, a negative quality that would make one lose face in the Greek-Roman world, opposite of a free person's demeanor;
3. pertains to being unpretentious, humble.[17]

Surprisingly, Jesus was telling the Jews that He was not overly impressed by a sense of self-importance. Instead, He considered Himself undistinguished and of low social status. He, the sovereign Creator of the universe, is humble and servile in manner. This is not how monarchs and rulers throughout history have viewed themselves, nor was it the perception of the Jews of Jesus' day of the Prophet-to-Come, their expected King. Kings are distinguished personages. They are not subservient; they rule, often ruthlessly. They are not lowly; they are exalted.

Jesus' gentleness and lowliness is exemplified in His astonishing humility. Not only did He leave a home that is more glorious than we will ever comprehend in this earthly life, He came as a nobody—not only a nobody, a servant. How low did our King of

---

16. Bauer, *Greek-English Lexicon*, 861 s.v. πραΰς.
17. Ibid., 989 s.v. ταπεινός 1, 2, 3.

8

The God of Equality

For by the grace given to me
I say to everyone among you
not to think of himself
more highly than he ought to think.[1]

◆ Paul to the church at Rome

IN HIS BOOK, *ANIMAL FARM*, George Orwell painted a disturbing allegorical picture of how a revolution led by farm animals—pigs, dogs, and horses—overthrew their human master and manipulated language and history in an attempt to gain their idealistic goals of equality and fairness. It wasn't long before one of their slogans was, "All animals are equal, but some animals are more equal than others."[2] For some reason, pigs thought they were more qualified to rule than all the other animals. Their naïve attempt at egalitarianism failed. Eventually the porcine leaders became no different—actually worse—than the farmer they replaced.

Mankind yearns for freedom and equality, and political, religious, and social movements through the centuries have arisen to give voice to that yearning. However, history teaches us that

1. Romans 12:3a.
2. Orwell, *Animal Farm,* chapter 10.

dominating human authority will almost always win out, rising up even in the very movements most dedicated to eliminate them. Yet, in spite of this often tragic historical reality, it has not been God's will to eliminate such systems, even those regimes we consider ruthless. Rulers infamous for their barbarity—too numerous to list here—have seized the reins of power and engineered the deaths of thousands, even millions of people.

We find such brutal despots in Scripture, as well. For example, in the Old Testament, we read about a heartless king, Nebuchadnezzar, who punished people by burning them alive or feeding them to wild beasts. Yet, Nebuchadnezzar's reign was established by God. When Daniel received the understanding of the king's dream, he rejoiced, saying, "Blessed be the name of God forever and ever, to whom belong wisdom and might. He changes times and seasons; *he removes kings and sets up kings.*"[3]

The New Testament echoes this view. Paul wrote without qualification, "Let every person be subject to the governing authorities. For there is no authority except from God, and those that exist have been instituted by God."[4]

However, although reigning monarchs may wield impressive and oppressive might, the institutions they rule mean very little to the God of the universe. Through Isaiah, the Lord majestically emphasized, "All the nations are as nothing before him, they are accounted by him as less than nothing and emptiness."[5]

Although the Lord allows them, earthly sovereign power means "less than nothing" to our great God. Instead, His loving, laser focus ultimately converges on our relationship with Him. Jesus came proclaiming, not the rise of another earthly kingdom, but a heavenly one with a heavenly Father. This kingdom would have room for only one king, and that ruler would not be a fallen man but a perfect God. However, that kingdom is yet to come. Until His return, the followers of Jesus are to be overseers in this kingdom, over which He reigns and will reign. However, because

---

3. Daniel 2:20–21a, italics added.
4. Romans 13:1.
5. Isaiah 40:17.

our relationship with the Father is His paramount concern and because He is all too aware of fallen mankind's lust for power, He tells His people to reject the world's intoxicating allure of might and authoritative ascendancy, which may damage both the one in command and the ones who are subject to those commands. The Lord God knows well the long history of our evil propensity to treat as nothing those over whom we have authority.

God's Kingdom Is One of Humble Equality

As we have read, Jesus taught that those who do not humble themselves and thereby become like powerless children would never enter the kingdom of God. This is a startling statement. "Never" is strong word, and it doesn't appear that Jesus is giving us any wiggle room in His assertion. However, the pronouncement about becoming children in order to enter God's kingdom should cause us to wonder what kind of rule Jesus was bringing. An empire of weakened children indicates that His kingdom is not characterized by the familiar earth-bound qualities of might and imposition of dominion over others, but rather by humility. To help give us insight about how the Lord views the use of power and rulership among His people, which are the defining characteristics of any kingdom, it will be instructive to look at a passage from the Old Testament.

The Lord's Instructions to the Kings of Israel

> When you come to the land that the Lord your God is giving you, and you possess it and dwell in it and then say, "I will set a king over me, like all the nations that are around me," you may indeed set a king over you whom the Lord your God will choose. One from among your brothers you shall set as king over you. You may not put a foreigner over you, who is not your brother. Only he must not acquire many horses for himself or cause the people

to return to Egypt in order to acquire many horses, since the LORD has said to you, "You shall never return that way again." And he shall not acquire many wives for himself, lest his heart turn away, nor shall he acquire for himself excessive silver and gold. And when he sits on the throne of his kingdom, he shall write for himself in a book a copy of this law, approved by the Levitical priests. And it shall be with him, and he shall read in it all the days of his life, that he may learn to fear the LORD his God by keeping all the words of this law and these statutes, and doing them, that his heart may not be lifted up above his brothers, and that he may not turn aside from the commandment, either to the right hand or to the left, so that he may continue long in his kingdom, he and his children, in Israel (Deuteronomy 17:14–20).

The Lord told Israel's kings to read the law all the days of their lives and keep it. Why did He command this? So they may "learn to fear the LORD," and that their hearts "may not be lifted up" above their brothers. This perception of rulership is strikingly different when compared to that of other sovereigns, both ancient and modern. There may be exceptions, but emperors and dictators did not and do not endeavor to find equality with their subjects. They seek to dominate them. Surely, God's admonition to Israel's kings was and still is an anomaly in the kingdoms of the world.

Lord Acton wrote, "Power tends to corrupt, and absolute power corrupts absolutely."[6] In our history, this statement appears to be true without refutation. God's knowledge of the corruptibility of the fallen nature of man is woven within the warp and woof of His instructions to Israel's kings. It was not His will for those monarchs to be corrupted, nor for His people to be ruined by that corruption. Thus, the Lord commanded these rulers to consider themselves as equals among their subjects. Yes, He allowed the kings of Israel to exist, although His people's demand for a king was a rejection of Him. This faithless refusal angered Him, and He warned Israel that those sovereigns would forcefully take their

---

6. Acton, *Historical Essays and Studies*, 504.

children and their goods.[7] Nevertheless, although the Lord permitted Israel's kings to be invested with the power of rulership, He demanded that their hearts not be lifted up above their brothers.

Think for a moment how easy it would have been for a king's heart to be exalted above his subjects. A king has power. In his own kingdom, he has all of the power. When he speaks, people obey. Things happen. This is not true of a farmer, merchant, or shepherd. Yes, he may have a certain authority in his family or occupation, but he does not possess an army with the ability to confiscate goods and exercise absolute rule over the general populace. When the king rides into a village with an armed guard, a common man's familial or occupational influence means very little. Everyone bows down and obsequiously gives the royal lord what he demands. If a king wants a farmer's crops, he seizes them. If he desires a merchant's wife, he abducts her. The poor man can do nothing about it. All power, including wealth, flow to the sovereign ruler. This is the way kingdoms have exercised authority, to one degree or another, since empires have existed. Perhaps it is more accurate to say that this dominance has been operative whenever superior earthly might has ruled over inferior power since man has walked the earth.

Do you think that supremacy might go to one's head?

Learning to Fear the Lord

To prevent the potential abuse of power, the Lord told Israel's kings to read the law all the days of their lives and keep it so they would learn to fear Him. Abiding in the Word of God would develop a fear of God in the hearts of His leaders as they read about the Lord's sovereign use of power in Israel's history. They would discover how awesomely formidable and wise He is, as well as how steadfastly loving and merciful. They would also find His laws supremely challenging, which should bring them to their knees in awe, humility, and repentance as they realized their inability to

---

[7]. 1 Samuel 8:1–18.

obey them. They would come to understand how desperately in need of the Lord's grace and mercy they were. They would also eventually come to know how lovely His law is, how perfect. Psalm 119 overbrims with declarations of the law's beauty: "Oh how I love your law! It is my meditation all the day."[8] The attaining of it in its fullness would be impossible, but it was and is, nevertheless, good and pure. His law is a statement of how holy and morally spotless God is, how high His standards are. Again, such knowledge should humble Israel's kings and cause His holy fear to grow and mature in their lives. Unfortunately, His Word was neglected and unread. After King Josiah had given instructions to repair the temple, Hilkiah found a book there and Shaphan brought it to the king with this stunning statement: "Hilkiah the priest has given me a book."[9] That "book" was the Word of God. It had been completely forgotten.

Fearing God Should Bring Humility to Rulers

Yet, how is fearing God related to a king of Israel not lifting up his heart above his brothers? When a ruler began to view himself as better than his brothers, he had turned away from the reality that he was a sinner and in need of God's mercy, just as his subjects were, and primary among those sins was the prideful use of power. He had reasoned that his elevated position was due to blood, superior human abilities, and political will, perhaps including clever, even brutal intrigue. He had concluded that God had chosen Him to reign by virtue of those gifts, not simply by His sovereign election. In addition, a king's pride in his position might cause him to take credit for his accomplishments, putting aside the central truth that God alone is supreme, not him. One outstanding example of this pride is the previously mentioned King Nebuchadnezzar, who, although not a king of Israel, was chosen by God. Notice the words "I" and "my" in his declaration as he walked on the roof of his

---

8. Psalm 119:97.
9. 2 Kings 22:10a.

royal palace in Babylon: "Is not this great Babylon, which I have built by my mighty power as a royal residence and for the glory of my majesty?"[10] Nebuchadnezzar would soon learn that he and the Lord had different views of the source of his sovereignty. Soon, he would be eating the grass of the field like an ox.[11]

Who removes and establishes kings and rulers? Only the Lord God Almighty. People may find themselves in high-ranking positions, as Nebuchadnezzar did, but are in error if they reason that standing has been achieved by virtue of their unique skill set or positional authority. Jesus told Pilate when He stood before him, "You would have no authority over me at all unless it had been given you from above."[12]

The Strange, Destructive Brew of Sovereign Power

The notion that a king considered himself better than his brothers flowed naturally from the inherent character of a hierarchical system. Regardless of who sat on the throne, the king of Israel would possess and exercise imperial power. He would *have* to exercise it: He was the sovereign. If he didn't prove himself strong, someone else would step into that power vacuum. The necessity to rule and accompanying might would produce a heady, intoxicating mix.

The Fall of Saul

An outstanding example of the exhilaration that power produces is the first king of Israel, Saul. After Samuel had anointed him to rule, Saul was so unsure of himself that he hid among the baggage when he realized that he had been chosen king.[13] Nevertheless, it was not long after Israel's defeat of the Amalekites that Saul set up a

10. Daniel 4:30.
11. Daniel 4:33
12. John 19:11a.
13. 1 Samuel 10:22.

monument for himself.[14] Thus, we see the amazingly short throw from a person's perceived insignificance to his self-exaltation when earthly accomplishments and its accompanying power are involved.

Earlier, when Saul and his army were under pressure from the gathering Philistine hordes, Saul offered the sacrifice before Samuel had arrived, although he had been clearly instructed to wait. Samuel then told him that he was being removed from office.[15] Why such strong discipline for a little impatience? Under pressure from the gathering Philistine host, Saul was disobedient and offered the sacrifice as a kind of pagan, good-luck sacrifice, like a shaman axing a chicken to "bless" a birth, marriage, or war. Saul could not be defeated in battle and maintain his political strength and position. He was compelled to act like a godless and faithless Gentile in order to keep his throne secure.

After the defeat of the Amalekites, Saul ignored the Lord's commands for a second time, and Samuel again informed Him that the Lord had rejected him as king of Israel. Saul explained to Samuel why he had not destroyed the Amalekites' animals but kept them to be offered as sacrifices instead: "I feared the people and obeyed their voice."[16] Again, Saul proceeded with actions that were religiously popular and politically expedient, even if it meant disobeying the Lord. And although we are not told why he spared Agag's life, it is my opinion that Saul did this because he was honoring the exalted position of this idol-worshiping despot as a member of the club of kings, so to speak.

The Lord removed Saul because he disobeyed His commands, desiring power and position more than obedience and godliness, stooping so low that he acted like a pagan himself. Saul succumbed to the potent intoxicant of sovereign human power.

---

14. 1 Samuel 15:12.
15. 1 Samuel 13:13–14.
16. 1 Samuel 15:24b.

The Sad Reigns of Israel's Kings

Most of the kings of Israel and Judah, with some notable exceptions, were either entranced by or abusive of their powers. Even David, the greatest of Israel's rulers and a man after God's heart, exploited his position by seizing and bedding the wife of another man. He sinned against God, mistreated Bathsheba by ripping apart her relationship with her husband, Uriah, and then committed the unconscionable act of murder by arranging his death. The sin-darkened accounts of Israel and Judah's reigning monarchs are stark examples of why the Lord told His kings to read the Word in order to fear Him and counteract the deleterious use of imperial power.

The Danger of Power Among Jesus' Disciples

Although the instructions in Deuteronomy 17 were clearly addressed to the kings of Israel and not to the Church, they should help us understand the Lord's heart concerning the use of earthly authority among His people. Jesus told His disciples that it was not His will that they rule as the world-wise Gentiles do: "A dispute also arose among them, as to which of them was to be regarded as the greatest. And he said to them, 'The kings of the Gentiles exercise lordship over them, and those in authority over them are called benefactors. But not so with you. Rather, let the greatest among you become as the youngest, and the leader as one who serves. For who is the greater, one who reclines at table or one who serves? Is it not the one who reclines at table? But I am among you as the one who serves.'"[17]

The Lord Jesus did not want His disciples to lead like this because He knew the ruinous effects of power on those who are in superior positions and those who are subject to them. He had witnessed that corruption in the long history of the world and His own people. He was fully aware of the possible dangers that would arise after His physical absence. After Jesus ascended, His disciples

---

17. Luke 22:24–27.

would be the only ones Jesus Himself had chosen. They were The Eleven. These men had been with Him during His ministering tenure on earth, traveled everywhere with Him, and witnessed Him healing the sick, raising the dead, delivering those possessed by demons, and working miracles. Only three of them had beheld Jesus glorified on the Mount of Transfiguration, and they alone were called by name to accompany Him when He went to pray on that dark, distressing night in Gethsemane. No one else had, not in Israel, not in the entire world. Therefore, these men would have tremendous authority. Like Israel's kings, they would be tempted to lift themselves up above their brothers. However, Jesus' disciples were chosen, not because of their inherent, superior giftedness or societal position, but only by God's gracious, sovereign will. None of them was in any way more exceptional than other men in Judea at that time.

The Danger of Power in the Church

The Church can learn from the Lord's admonitions to the kings of Israel in Deuteronomy 17, as well as those to His disciples in Luke 22. We must be cautious in our use of power, as well, and not allow our hearts to be lifted up above our brothers and sisters. A sense of superiority may naturally develop in us simply because power is systemically embedded in a religious organization. It is not the kind of power that kings wield, but it is a power over others, nonetheless.[18] It is a potentially dangerous place to reside. Just ask the most righteous king who ever reigned in the history of Israel.

---

18. The sovereign use of earthly, king-like power has been exercised by religious leaders throughout the history of the Church. Tragically, it was within two centuries after the lives of Jesus and the apostles that the Church began to appropriate secular power, which budded into flower under the Roman emperor Constantine. The author recommends reading a history of the Church.

The Apostle Paul and the Equality of Leaders

The apostle Paul echoed the Lord's admonition concerning the equality of leaders in his letter to the church at Corinth. The believers in that city were divided because some were choosing one leader over another. Paul told them, therefore, that they were infants in Christ and people of the flesh and then wrote, "For when one says, 'I follow Paul,' and another, 'I follow Apollos,' are you not being merely human? What then is Apollos? What is Paul? Servants through whom you believed, as the Lord assigned to each. I planted, Apollos watered, but God gave the growth. So neither he who plants nor he who waters is anything, but only God who gives the growth. He who plants and he who waters are one, and each will receive his wages according to his labor."[19]

Please take note of what Paul stated:

He and Apollos were servants.

He planted, and Apollos watered; but neither one of them was "anything." In other words, they were nothing, in no way worthy of note or superior to anyone else.

God gave the growth, but Paul did not cause anything to grow and neither did Apollos.

Paul and Apollos were "one," which means that neither of them was distinguishable from the other. They were equals—equals in servitude, in fact: "What then is Apollos? What is Paul? Servants through whom you believed, as the Lord assigned to each."

If Christians consider certain leaders greater than others, we come under Paul's scathing rebuke. We are infants in Christ, people of the flesh. Pastors and leaders, according to Paul, are not personalities whom we are to follow only because their ministries have grown, because as Paul clearly wrote, only God "gives the growth." They are "not anything." They are co-equal servants of God with everyone else.

---

19. 1 Corinthians 3:1, 4–8.

The God of Equality

Romans Twelve and the Equality of Gifted Believers

Paul, by the Holy Spirit, reiterated the Lord's heart concerning equality among believers to the church in Rome: "I appeal to you therefore, brothers, by the mercies of God, to present your bodies as a living sacrifice, holy and acceptable to God, which is your spiritual worship. Do not be conformed to this world, but be transformed by the renewal of your mind, that by testing you may discern what is the will of God, what is good and acceptable and perfect. For by the grace given to me I say to everyone among you *not to think of himself more highly than he ought to think*, but to think with sober judgment, each according to the measure of faith that God has assigned. For as in one body we have many members, and the members do not all have the same function, so we, though many, are one body in Christ, and individually members one of another."[20]

Sometimes, we stop at the first two verses or do not connect them with the portion that follows. However, we must connect them, since verse three begins with the word "for," which means that the truths that have preceded are going to be explained and clarified by the verses that follow. Therefore, if we read this entire passage in context, we will understand that offering our bodies in spiritual worship, not conforming to the world, and being transformed by the renewing of our minds means not ranking oneself above other believers in a stratified structure of significance, which is the way of a world that lusts for preeminence. Paul is again connecting God's admonition to Israel concerning her kings in Deuteronomy: Do not let your hearts be lifted up above your brothers.

Why should we not think more highly of ourselves than we ought? Because, Paul wrote: "For as in one body we have many members, and the members do not all have the same function, so we, though many, are one body in Christ, and individually members one of another."[21]

---

20. Romans 12:1–5, italics added.
21. Romans 12:4–5.

Then, to help the Roman believers understand the practical implications of this equality, he told them how to view their ministries: "Having gifts that differ according to the grace given to us, let us use them: if prophecy, in proportion to our faith; if service, in our serving; the one who teaches, in his teaching; the one who exhorts, in his exhortation; the one who contributes, in generosity; the one who leads, with zeal; the one who does acts of mercy, with cheerfulness."[22]

Paul is telling the church at Rome that if there were prophets among their number, those prophets should exercise that gift in faith but not think of themselves as any better than anyone else in the church and seek a place of prominence. They should not forget that God once spoke through a donkey. He also spoke through Balaam, who led Israel into error and was killed for that transgression. God chooses people for one reason: the counsel of His own gracious will. Therefore, prophets should pursue humility. There is not anything special about them, nor are they more spiritual or better than others.

Were there those in the church at Rome who possessed the gift of service? This is a beautiful calling, given by God's grace. However, these Christians should not get haughty and begin thinking they are the true servants of God while others are not. Remember Martha?

Were there teachers? These gifted men and women should do their best to show themselves approved, workers who have no need to be ashamed, as Paul instructed Timothy. However, they should not lift themselves above others by virtue of their knowledge of Scripture or ability to communicate.

Did God give some in the church at Rome the grace to give generously? This is a vital gift to help those in need. However, these benevolent believers should be careful about becoming critical of others who, according to their ascetic lights, spend too much money on themselves. They would need to avoid thinking they are clearly superior due to their care for the poor.

---

22. Romans 12:6–8.

Did the Lord give some the gift of mercy? What a gracious gift! These Christians may find it easier to show compassion than others, but they must avoid considering themselves better than those who are yet growing in kindness and empathy.

A Similar Situation in Corinth

Paul dealt with the same pride-in-giftedness problem in the church at Corinth. He instructed those believers how to regard those who possess spiritual gifts given by a gracious God, reminding them they were members of one another. None were superstars, and none were inessential unknowns.[23] The passage below is reminiscent of what we read earlier in Romans 12, where Paul wrote that we should not think more highly of ourselves than we ought to think. That wrong-headed perception of giftedness is being conformed to the way the world thinks. "On the contrary, the parts of the body that seem to be weaker are indispensable, and on those parts of the body that we think less honorable we bestow the greater honor, and our unpresentable parts are treated with greater modesty, which our more presentable parts do not require. But God has so composed the body, giving greater honor to the part that lacked it, that there may be no division in the body, but that the members may have the same care for one another. If one member suffers, all suffer together; if one member is honored, all rejoice together."[24]

Do we want to know our glorious Lord God of love and not be conformed to the world? One way is to give greater honor to those who have none, who do not deserve any according to our perception of honor. On which part of the body are we to give greater honor? Gifted believers? No. The weaker members. We are to give greater honor to "the part that lacked it." Why? So that there is no division in the body, Paul wrote, and that we all have the same care for one another. No one is more important than another. In

---

23. 1 Corinthians 12:11–21.
24. 1 Corinthians 12:22–26.

fact, the members who have the least honor should receive *more* of our honoring attention than the ones who, if we think as the world thinks (and, unfortunately, we often do), seem to be most important among us. When significant people lift up those who are perceived as less significant, it humbles the elevated and exalts the lowly. This will help instill a view of equality among Christian believers, so their hearts will not be lifted up above their brothers and sisters.

The God of Equality and the Lord's Supper

Paul's admonitions to the church in 1 Corinthians 12 follow his teaching on the Lord's Supper in chapter 11, where he was dealing with a similar issue concerning pride of position. In this part of the letter, the apostle was very unhappy with the Corinthians because they were pushing ahead of each other and even getting drunk when they came together at table. "For in eating, each one goes ahead with his own meal. One goes hungry, another gets drunk. What! Do you not have houses to eat and drink in? Or do you despise the church of God and humiliate those who have nothing? What shall I say to you? Shall I commend you in this? No, I will not."[25]

Note the question that Paul asked in these verses: "Or do you despise the church of God and *humiliate those who have nothing?*"[26] The Corinthians were giving preference to those who were important or rich by the world's standards and humiliating those who were poor. They did not understand the nature of the body of Christ nor God's heart concerning value and standing.

Verse 22 ends with this question and statement: "Shall I commend you in this? No, I will not." This was Paul telling the Corinthians that they had failed when they came together to partake of the Lord's Supper. His question and statement are followed by this passage: "For I received from the Lord what I also delivered to you, that the Lord Jesus on the night when he was betrayed took

---

25. 1 Corinthians 11:21–22.
26. 1 Corinthians 11:22a, italics added.

bread, and when he had given thanks, he broke it, and said, 'This is my body which is for you. Do this in remembrance of me.' In the same way also he took the cup, after supper, saying, 'This cup is the new covenant in my blood. Do this, as often as you drink it, in remembrance of me.' For as often as you eat this bread and drink the cup, you proclaim the Lord's death until he comes."[27]

Was Jesus—the humble and sacrificial God—being remembered and honored by the Corinthians as they broke bread in communion?

Please notice that the second word of the next portion is "therefore." Paul remains in context here. He is still writing about the body of Christ and how the members of the Corinthian church behave toward each other. The verses read: "Whoever, therefore, eats the bread or drinks the cup of the Lord in an unworthy manner will be guilty concerning the body and blood of the LORD. Let a person examine himself, then, and so eat of the bread and drink of the cup. For anyone who eats and drinks without discerning the body eats and drinks judgment on himself. That is why many of you are weak and ill, and some have died. But if we judged ourselves truly, we would not be judged. But when we are judged by the Lord, we are disciplined so that we may not be condemned along with the world."[28]

Paul was telling the Corinthians that they were drinking the cup in an unworthy manner because they were not discerning the body. "For anyone who eats and drinks without discerning the body eats and drinks judgment on himself."[29] He was also informing them, stunningly, that many were weak and ill and that some had even died because of their lack of discernment. This statement is extraordinary. Nothing can be added by this author except an exhortation to realize that the issue of equality among believers is enormously more important than we know. To ignore it invites spiritual catastrophe.

---

27. 1 Corinthians 11:23–26.
28. 1 Corinthians 11:27–32.
29. 1 Corinthians 11:29.

The God We Do Not Know

The God of Equality

The Christian God is a God of equality. He views all of His followers without distinction, regardless of giftedness, wealth, influence, or position. He expects us to do the same. This is not how people in the world think of themselves and of others, but we are not to be conformed to that world. It is not debatable that throughout history we in the Church have abused hierarchical power and still do. That positional authority is too often destructive, and God's desire is to subdue it. Christians are to be equals, and there should not be any notion of superior individuals in the Church. We begin to inculcate this unlike-the-world perception into our lives by knowing His truth in the Word and fearing Him. He alone dwells in heaven and is sovereign over all. None of us can make that claim. He alone is exalted. We are equals. He alone is worthy of glory. No man or woman is. He alone has a name that is holy. We are all disastrously, sinfully unholy and in need of His righteousness. He is a God to be feared, and men and women are not.

He is the God of equality.

He is the God we do not know.

9

The God of Fear

*And do not fear those who kill the body
but cannot kill the soul.
Rather fear him who can destroy
both soul and body in hell.*[1]

~ Jesus to His disciples

LAURIE AND I ARRIVED on a late-night flight out of Hong Kong into Port Moresby, Papua New Guinea, one of the most dangerous cities on earth. Disheveled and jet-lagged after a twenty-four hour trip from the United States, we were met at the airport and whisked away in a van to the walled compound of our denomination's headquarters. After mutual introductions and conversation ensued in the pastor's living room, a smiling, stout man rushed in bearing exciting news. A drunken fellow had slipped into the compound when we came through the gate, he told us. Christians on the night watch had seized this intruder, but he fought them. So, the guards found it necessary to administer some punitive measures in order to subdue him. They then spent some time sharing the good news about Jesus. The security guard explained that

---

1. Matthew 10:28.

after hearing the gospel, the man said, "When I first came in, I was confused. But now that you have hit me, I see things more clearly."

Welcome to Papua New Guinea. Some might say that these men had "put the fear of God" into this wayward man.

Within a year, however, I was subjected to a fear in this country of an entirely different kind.

Early one morning as I was praying, I suddenly experienced a dread that sent me sprawling. This was not the fear of a child terrified of monsters in the dark nor of an adult alone in a parking lot at night. I was not at all afraid of dying or being hurt. I saw nothing. I heard nothing. But the source of the distress was indisputable. The sovereign fear of God had arrived in our tin-roofed apartment, and it was real and overwhelming. I got down on my hands and knees and lowered my forehead to the ground. That was really all I was able to do. I was so overcome that I pleaded with the Lord, telling Him I could endure it no more. Gradually, the fear dissipated.

Looking back, I thank the Lord for that wondrous, terror-inducing time because I know now that the biblical fear of God is not a vague, insipid reverence.

It is soul-shaking, as it should be.

Such dramatic events are not necessary for Christians to believe that their God is a God of fear. However, frightening encounters with the Lord are biblical, and we can learn from them, as well. Daniel, Ezekiel, Paul, and John were all confronted by a glorious reality that brought them to their knees. Isaiah was similarly undone when confronted with the holy God and cried "Woe is me! For I am lost; for I am a man of unclean lips, and I dwell in the midst of a people of unclean lips; for my eyes have seen the King, the Lord of hosts!"[2]

The word "lost" is rendered in other translations as "ruined," "undone," or "destroyed." Like these men, and others throughout Church history, I was profoundly aware that the holy Lord God was making His glorious presence known—and that I was a very unholy, inglorious man.

---

2. Isaiah 6:5.

The God of Fear

Biblical Fear

The Bible teaches us that the fear of God is a necessary part of a believer's life.

Solomon taught that "if we seek wisdom and understanding like silver, like hidden treasure, we would come to understand the fear of the Lord and find the knowledge of God."[3]

When Jethro advised Moses about which men to choose to assist him judge the people, he said, "Moreover, look for able men from all the people, men who fear God, who are trustworthy and hate a bribe, and place such men over the people as chiefs of thousands, of hundreds, of fifties, and of tens."[4]

Fearing God is connected with moral, obedient behavior but is also intermingled with loving Him, as Deuteronomy 10:12-13 says: "And now, Israel, what does the LORD your God require of you, but to fear the LORD your God, to walk in all his ways, to love him, to serve the LORD your God with all your heart and with all your soul, and to keep the commandments and statutes of the LORD, which I am commanding you today for your good?"

The Fear of God in the New Testament

However, is the fear of the Lord only an aspect of a blessings-and-cursings Old-Testament covenant that has been fulfilled and replaced?

Paul told us to fear God, quoting the prophet Isaiah: "'I will make my dwelling among them and walk among them, and I will be their God, and they shall be my people. Therefore go out from their midst, and be separate from them, says the Lord, and touch no unclean thing; then I will welcome you, and I will be a father to you, and you shall be sons and daughters to me, says the Lord Almighty.' Since we have these promises, beloved, let us cleanse

---

3. Proverbs 2:4-5.
4. Exodus 18:21.

ourselves from every defilement of body and spirit, bringing holiness to completion in the fear of God."[5]

The Lord declared He will be a father to us. However, since we have this promise, Paul warned, we should "cleanse ourselves from every defilement" in the "fear of God." According to these Spirit-inspired words, the fear of the Lord remains co-mingled with love, obedience, and upright behavior in the New Testament.

A Covenant of Fear

Perhaps we may gain better understanding of this holy fear by investigating what the Lord told His people through Malachi. When the prophet Malachi arrived on the scene, he spoke unsettling words to the people of Israel. Ezra had come and demanded that the Jews put away their foreign wives. Nehemiah also brought spiritual reform and oversaw the rebuilding of the walls of Jerusalem. However, after all the reforms, after all the promises, Malachi discovered that Judah had fallen back into pagan ways and "married the daughter of a foreign god."[6] The priests had offered lame, sick, and blind animals as sacrifices.[7] Their ministry seemed a meaningless drudgery. "What a weariness this is," they complained.[8] The Lord rebuked them and compared the current priesthood to the original one: "My covenant with him was one of life and peace, and I gave them to him. It was a covenant of fear, and he feared me. He stood in awe of my name. True instruction was in his mouth, and no wrong was found on his lips. He walked with me in peace and uprightness, and he turned many from iniquity."[9]

The Lord asserted that His covenant with Levi was one of life and peace. However, immediately following, He said, "It was a covenant of fear, and he feared me."

---

5. 2 Corinthians 6:16b—7:1.
6. Malachi 2:11.
7. Malachi 1:8.
8. Malachi 1:13.
9. Malachi 2:5–6.

How do life, peace, and fear co-exist? Can fear ever be peaceful? Solomon wrote in Proverbs 14:27, "The fear of the Lord is a fountain of life, that one may turn away from the snares of death." Fearing God is life-giving? How do we combine these two seemingly contrasting truths?

Jesus presented this same, puzzling contrast when He warned about persecution and said, "So have no fear of them, for nothing is covered that will not be revealed, or hidden that will not be known. What I tell you in the dark, say in the light, and what you hear whispered, proclaim on the housetops. And do not fear those who kill the body but cannot kill the soul. Rather fear him who can destroy both soul and body in hell. Are not two sparrows sold for a penny? And not one of them will fall to the ground apart from your Father. But even the hairs of your head are all numbered. Fear not, therefore; you are of more value than many sparrows. So everyone who acknowledges me before men, I also will acknowledge before my Father who is in heaven, but whoever denies me before men, I also will deny before my Father who is in heaven."[10]

Do not fear men, Jesus taught, even when they want to kill you.

Instead, fear the Father, who can throw you into hell.

However, He added, you are of great value.

But do not deny Him, Jesus warned, or He will deny you before the Father.

Perplexed? We should be.

The Words of Those Who Fear Him

Perhaps we may gain further insight by looking at another passage from Malachi. After the Lord had rebuked Israel, foretold the coming of his messenger, and rebuked them again for robbing Him because of their lack of generosity, some of His people took seriously what He said: "Then those who feared the Lord spoke with one another. The Lord paid attention and heard them, and a book

---

10. Matthew 10:26–33.

of remembrance was written before him of those who feared the LORD and esteemed his name. 'They shall be mine, says the LORD of hosts, in the day when I make up my treasured possession, and I will spare them as a man spares his son who serves him. Then once more you shall see the distinction between the righteous and the wicked, between one who serves God and one who does not serve him.'"[11]

The Lord "paid attention" to the conversation of those who feared Him. Something was written down in a book as they spoke. They shall be His, the Lord said, in the day when He makes up His "treasured possession."

God Takes Notes

When I was writing this chapter, I had coffee one morning with a friend and discussed the difficulty I had wrapping my mind around the things I was learning about the fear of God—how fear, obedience, and love were intertwined. I read the passage from Malachi and said, "Gary, right now, the Lord is listening to the words we're speaking and writing something down about them in a book." We both paused, startled by a holy reality. The Lord God Almighty was listening to our conversation at that very moment.

And taking notes.

So, a question that may further our understanding of godly fear: How will it be for you when you stand before Him, and He looks into His book to find your conversations about fearing Him?

This verse should continue to renew a healthy fear of that moment: "And now, little children, abide in him, so that when he appears we may have confidence and not shrink from him in shame at his coming."[12]

Perhaps this is not important to us. However, if that is the case, we do not understand the overwhelming glory and majesty of the Lord of all things.

---

11. Malachi 3:16–18.
12. 1 John 2:28.

The God of Fear

The Fear of the Lord Is Clean

In this beautiful psalm, David wrote that the fear of the Lord is "clean."

> The law of the LORD is perfect,
> reviving the soul;
> the testimony of the LORD is sure,
> making wise the simple;
> the precepts of the LORD are right,
> rejoicing the heart;
> the commandment of the LORD is pure,
> enlightening the eyes;
> the fear of the LORD is clean,
> enduring forever;
> the rules of the LORD are true,
> and righteous altogether.
> More to be desired are they than gold,
> even much fine gold;
> sweeter also than honey
> and drippings of the honeycomb.
> Moreover, by them is your servant warned;
> in keeping them there is great reward
> (Psalm 19:7–11).

The fear of the Lord is clean. Clear. If we have life in Him and know Him; if we abide in His love, we want to obey and do right—we love to obey. We fear displeasing the God who gave His life for us. This is straightforward—simple.

David was elegantly uncomplicated when he wrote:

> Let the words of my mouth
> and the meditation of my heart

The God We Do Not Know

> be acceptable in your sight, O Lord,
> my rock and my redeemer.
> (Psalm 19:14).

It was plain to David. He did not want to sin against his beloved Lord. He knew he was accountable for the words he spoke and desired that they were acceptable to the Lord; yes, even the meditation of his heart. He did not want to displease Him. Paul also wrote of his desire to please his God and King: "So whether we are at home or away, we make it our aim to please him. For we must all appear before the judgment seat of Christ, so that each one may receive what is due for what he has done in the body, whether good or evil."[13]

We should tremble at the thought that we, if we profess Christ, will be found wanting when we stand before Him, risking His displeasure.

However, in that displeasure, in that fear, He loves us. So, let us be unambiguous. For Christians, the fear of God is not the dread of eternal damnation. That punishment was absorbed by Jesus in His atoning sacrifice. Fear of the Lord for those who know and follow Jesus is a deep, life-encompassing awe for the God who created us and cherishes us; a God whom we love and profoundly respect down to the root core of who we are as Christians, because He, the most powerful being imaginable, first loved us.

John wrote, "God is love, and whoever abides in love abides in God, and God abides in him. By this is love perfected with us, so that we may have confidence for the day of judgment, because as he is so also are we in this world. There is no fear in love, but perfect love casts out fear. For fear has to do with punishment, and whoever fears has not been perfected in love. We love because he first loved us."[14]

The Word of God is unequivocal on this point. Perfect love casts out fear. Dread of punishment is to be thrown forcefully away. However, we need to comprehend what "perfect" love is.

---

13. 2 Corinthians 5:9–10.
14. 1 John 4:16b–19.

Perfect, complete love is a love that wraps itself around a biblical abhorrence of displeasing the almighty Creator God who was mocked and slaughtered like a worthless criminal for us. Thus, as love is perfected, we have confidence on the Day of Judgment, but fear remains, as John wrote, of shrinking back from Him in shame before the Judgment Seat of Christ.

It is foolish for me to write this, but I must.

God is brilliantly difficult to comprehend.

However, we are not alone in our perplexity. David exclaimed:

> O LORD, you have searched me and known me!
> You know when I sit down and when I rise up;
> you discern my thoughts from afar.
> You search out my path and my lying down
> and are acquainted with all my ways.
> Even before a word is on my tongue, behold, O LORD,
> you know it altogether. You hem me in,
> behind and before, and lay your hand upon me.
> Such knowledge is too wonderful for me;
> it is high; I cannot attain it (Psalm 139:1–6).

Followers of Jesus Christ are to fear and obey the God who created and reigns over them and all the staggering totality of creation—a gloria mundi of bewilderment and love.

He is the God we do not know.

10

The God of Love

We love because he first loved us.[1]

～ The Apostle John

OVER TWO THOUSAND YEARS ago, a woman—a prostitute—boldly disrupted a dinner attended by a roomful of religious men. Pressing past social and religious norms, ignoring the discomfort, guilt, and shame, she stood behind a man, her Savior, and wept with such gut-wrenching intensity that she bathed His feet with her tears.[2]

This was true emotion indeed.

This was true love indeed.

Rebels push back against outdated stigmas and social mores, but no rebellion arose here. This "woman of the city," as Luke called her, was driven by a force she could no longer deny: the overwhelming love of the God she had not known. Had she witnessed that love in action when Jesus ministered to the sick, the lame, and the blind? Perhaps she had watched in wonder as He forgave the woman taken in adultery. The Holy Spirit convinced her in those moments that the divine love she needed and longed

---

1. 1 John 4:19.
2. Luke 7:36–38.

for was resident in this Man. Nothing, including her own personal humiliation, would keep her away.

God's love, once known, once experienced, is irresistible. It compels us to come to Him.

God's Love for Those He Created

The Lord God Almighty created human beings in the likeness of Himself, a holy and perfect God, without evil, perversion, or betrayal. Not long after He did so, the people He created in His majestic image began to engage in the most heinous deeds imaginable. They hated, killed, raped, and burned alive those whom He had fearfully and wonderfully knitted together in their mothers' wombs. They took advantage of the weak and vulnerable, crushing their necks under their feet. Multitudes foolishly worshiped lifeless idols of metal, wood, and stone. Soon, His human creations told Him they did not believe in Him; some proclaimed that He did not even exist. Others blasphemed His name, trampling it in the mud as if it were dung. These evils "grieved him to his heart."[3] What should this all-powerful God do? He regretted that He had even created mankind and subsequently punished them. Nevertheless, for millennia His own creations continued to ignore and rebel against Him. Eventually, He revealed His exquisite, unimaginable solution: He Himself would die for their terrible sins and unbelief, absorbing the punishment He could have poured out upon them for the rejection of their Creator.

This He did in Jesus. Sins, evil, and rebellion may be forgiven. The slate of shame can be wiped clean. We may now know Him and fellowship with Him. Once unholy sinners, believers in Jesus Christ have been given His righteousness, the righteousness of God Himself. "For our sake he made him to be sin who knew no sin, so that in him we might become the righteousness of God."[4]

---

3. Genesis 6:6.
4. 2 Corinthians 5:21.

However, that is not all. These horrible, debased ones—He adopts them. He brings them into His family. He makes these fallen creations, of all improbable things, His sons and daughters. He gives them a share in the eternal inheritance He has for His Son, the One who is holy and full of glory. "Blessed be the God and Father of our Lord Jesus Christ! According to his great mercy, he has caused us to be born again to a living hope through the resurrection of Jesus Christ from the dead, to an inheritance that is imperishable, undefiled, and unfading, kept in heaven for you, who by God's power are being guarded through faith for a salvation ready to be revealed in the last time."[5]

What they deserved—punishment—He took into Himself. He was mocked. Whipped like a dog. Executed like a despised murderer, fastened to a cross with cruel, iron spikes. Slaughtered like a little, helpless lamb.

What His creations did not deserve—His nature, His holy righteousness, His possessions—He gave to them.

This is what the Almighty God did.

This is why we love Him. This is why we serve and obey Him.

The God of New Creations

Scripture announces the stunning news that once a person believes in Jesus Christ, God, incomprehensibly, creates a new human being—spiritually.[6] No one except the Lord knows how this miraculous act of love is done. One day you are a spiritually lost and blind sinner, and the next you are changed into an individual who, although not perfect, begins to lose the affection you once had for a dark, dying world and its shameful attractions. Your life changes; you desire activities you swore you never would. You are hungry to be taught the truth in the Bible, which now is wonderfully attractive to you. You want to be around and talk to "the people of the book," as one Chinese woman referred to Christians

---

5. 1 Peter 1:3–5.
6. 2 Corinthians 5:17.

when she told us her tale of salvation. You ache as she did to know and pray to this remarkable God that you once thought was just an ideology, an energy, a force in nature. You now know that He is personal, real.

And that your almighty Creator loves you.

The God of Love, The God of Power

The loving Christian God is a God of unsurpassed might. He exists within a formidable primacy that is wholly unfathomable to us. It's a wonderful thing, is it not, that the God who has the ability to create and do anything He pleases with just a word, is also your Friend and Father? Shouldn't we greatly rejoice that this omnipotent God, who could capriciously toss our entire planet into the icy, deadness of space, instead, loves us—and will love us forever? Shouldn't we fall to our knees in adoration when we consider that what lies ahead for those who believe Him is a joyful, glorious residence for ten trillion times ten trillion years and more?

Christian Forgiveness

The Lord God of all things, the God of unsurpassed might, is not a grim and ruthless potentate who thrills in the destruction of those who oppose Him. He loves. He is patient. He forgives. And He expects us to forgive, as well. Jesus made it clear in the parable of the unforgiving servant that unforgiveness brings no joyful outcome.[7] Below is a stunning account about a violent soldier who exhibited forgiveness for those who had attempted to murder him.

Eric Karua, an associate pastor and musician from Papua New Guinea, is a friend of mine. Before Eric became a Christian, he was a very angry, hard-hearted, and violent man. When the Solomon Islands fought for independence from Papua New Guinea, he enlisted as a soldier with the Bougainville Resistance Army. But at some point, the Resistance Army divided, and the two factions

---

7. Matthew 18:32–35.

began to fight each other. The war for independence had become a civil war. Eric joined the newly formed Bougainville Resistance Force. Sadly, that civil war, as do many such conflicts, pitted village against village, family against family and brother against brother. In fact, Eric told me he once put a gun to his wife's head when he thought she was betraying him to her family. As I said, he was an angry man.

One night he decided that he would go to his wife's village to visit her. He asked a couple of his friends to go with him, but they were too afraid; so he went alone. Eric was on a dark, jungle road, carrying an M-16, three extra magazines in his cargo pockets. Two grenades hung from his belt.

Suddenly a man grabbed him from behind, wrapping his arms around him.

"I've got him!" he shouted.

Eric quickly brought up his M-16 and began spraying the areas in front of and beside him. When he exhausted the magazine, he tried to reach into his pocket to retrieve a full one. By this time, however, another man had begun to stab him repeatedly, in his chest, neck, and head. Finally, Eric was stabbed in the back, near his kidneys, and he fell unconscious. When he came to, he heard the commander of the group say, "Finish him off."

The attacker aimed his weapon at Eric, who was certain his death was just moments away. For the first time in his life, he prayed, "God, save me. Don't let me die." The assailant fired, but the round misfired. He ejected it and tried another. It was a dud, too, as was the third one.

Finally, the commander said, "Leave him to die."

Eric regained and lost consciousness three times. Each time, he felt himself falling into a dark and bottomless pit.

Eventually, he gathered his strength and crawled to the house of friend. When he arrived at the front door, he called out twice, "Steven." The third time, when he opened his mouth, nothing came out. He dragged himself to another house. On the way, however, he saw a Coleman lantern hanging inside a church. As he drew nearer, the light became smaller and smaller, until it was the size of a firefly. Eric was dying.

The people in the church were praying and had their eyes closed. Eric crawled to the pulpit and grabbed it. When the pastor felt the pulpit move, he looked down, but Eric was so bloody he didn't recognize him. The pastor took off his own shirt and wiped the blood from Eric's face. The people quickly realized the extent of Eric's wounds, and it wasn't long before he was on his way to a hospital. He had almost bled to death. He had to undergo surgery to stop the internal bleeding and spent a month in bed, but he eventually recovered.

It was during this time and afterward that Eric fully gave his heart to Jesus Christ and began to preach the Gospel. Everyone, including his wife, Sarah, was amazed at how this hardened man had changed. However, although Eric was doing a lot of ministering, his heart was still full of bitterness and hatred toward the man who had attacked him so brutally. When he decided to go to this man and tell him that he had forgiven him, none of his village friends or family would go with him. They gave him a new M-16 and urged him to take it with him, but he refused.

By the time Eric arrived, word had spread that he was coming. He went into the man's house, which by then was surrounded by soldiers who were ready to kill him at the first misstep. Eric found his enemy sleeping. When he nudged him awake, the man went for his weapon, the M-16 he had taken from Eric the night of the attack.

Eric put his hand out and said, "No, I haven't come to fight. Enough people have died. I have come to forgive you for what you've done."

Eric immediately felt released from his bitterness. Then his enemy broke down and cried. This man told Eric that he had free access to come and preach to the people in his village and that he wouldn't be harmed.

However, this isn't the end of the story. Eric's family had sent his fourteen-year-old brother to school in an area in the north where it was safe. Eric had made so many enemies that they, in retribution, sought out his younger brother and murdered him. Eric found himself at another crossroad. His friends and family wanted revenge. However, even though he was tempted, Eric wouldn't do it. By God's grace, he was able to forgive, again, in the realization that bloodshed and payback hadn't brought anything but more pain and death. When the time came for the first steps toward peace, the laying down of arms, Eric's village was the first to do so.[8]

Forgiveness is often a formidable task. We have been hurt and offended; betrayed. Our desire for revenge seems justified. However, as difficult as it is, Scripture does not offer sympathy with our struggle to obey this command. The reason it does not is because we have betrayed, dishonored, and disbelieved the innocent Creator and holy Lord of all that exists—and often still do. He is therefore the most justified in accusing and condemning us.

Yet, He forgives.

The Love Chapter

First Corinthians 13 presents Christians, and all people, with remarkable truths about the love of God. The chapter is remarkable because we see the beautiful reality of a God who is so good, so perfect, so rock-solid right.

And so unlike us. We discover in these few verses how far we fall short when we compare God's love with ours. Nevertheless, in spite of our inability to reach the Lord's unreachable standards, Paul exhorts the Corinthians—and us—to portray His amazing love to each other and to the world.

God's Love Is Patient

Paul begins by writing that God's love is patient.[9] The Lord is long-suffering as we fail to do what we know is right and good, put

---

8. Thomson, *Deeper*, 85–88.
9. 1 Corinthians 13:4.

our trust in people or things instead of Him, act or speak in ways that are shameful, or even betray or deny Him. In other words, God is patient with us as we slowly, so very slowly, even painfully, it seems, grow in our life with Him. Love is a fruit of the Spirit. Fruit does not grow and mature overnight, as nature plainly reveals.

Thus, all too often, we find it difficult to exhibit tolerance with others when they fail and sin. Instead, we may hastily arrive at the conclusion that they just don't get it. They do not change fast enough—like we would, of course. In addition, we are sometimes much too quick to make negative and critical determinations about people based upon a relatively short snapshot of their lives. More than likely, we do not know what caused these sons and daughters of fallen Adam to arrive at what we see as a deplorable state. If we knew, we would be more careful to view them with compassion and thus support them as they work and heal, with God's help, through the debilitating effects of sin. Paul wrote, "We who are strong have an obligation to bear with the failings of the weak, and not to please ourselves. Let each of us please his neighbor for his good, to build him up."[10]

In addition, since we are not God, you and I have no knowledge about what gracious act the Lord may do in a person's life some day in the future. We are unaware of what divine event must transpire as He patiently draws an individual to the truth, to Himself. The Lord does not always react to sin immediately and punish people for their disastrous behavior. And aren't we glad that He doesn't? We once were like those with whom we are now so impatient. Well, truthfully, we still are. If we say we have no sin, the Apostle John wrote, we are not telling the truth.[11]

---

10. Romans 15:1–2.
11. 1 John 1:8

God's Love Is Kind

The Greek word "kind," *chrēsteúomai*, is defined as "To be kind, obliging, willing to help or assist."[12] Kindness naturally follows the consideration of His patience with us. Our natural human reaction to objectionable behavior is to shun, reject, or condemn people. I once heard the testimony from a woman who had lived a notorious, sin-embedded life and had come to know Jesus simply because a pastor and his wife had invited her to dinner and kindly told her about the God who loved her and died for her. She did not expect such heartfelt care and lack of judgmentalism. I do not know if her perception was shaped by unfortunate encounters with believers or a false understanding of true Christian behavior; regardless, followers of Jesus should be cognizant of the difficulty we have being kind to blatant, active sinners—both those in the faith and those who are not. Since Paul began this chapter about love by stating, "If I speak in the tongues of men and of angels, but have not love, I am a noisy gong or a clanging cymbal," perhaps it's not a stretch to say that if we speak the language of Christianity without love and kindness, we likewise are also just a grating babble of biblical truths. Jesus commanded us to love even our enemies, those who do not deserve kindness at all: "But love your enemies, and do good, and lend, expecting nothing in return, and your reward will be great, and you will be sons of the Most High, for he is kind to the ungrateful and the evil. Be merciful, even as your Father is merciful."[13]

Our loving God, even though we are too often unkind to others, is kind to us and stands willing to help us in our struggle to conform ourselves to His nature, as we slowly discover that it is His kindness, not hard-heartedness, that leads saint and sinner alike to repentance.[14]

---

12. Zodhiates, *Complete Word Study*, see #5541 χρηστεύομαι *chrēsteúomai*.
13. Luke 6:35–36.
14. Romans 2:4.

The God of Love

God's Love Is Not Envious

Envy does not exist in the heart of God because He possesses everything in the universe. No one, no living entity, can make such a claim. He alone needs nothing whatsoever from us or His creation. "Behold, to the Lord your God belong heaven and the heaven of heavens, the earth with all that is in it."[15]

Nothing exists that the Lord does not own, including the dirt, the stone, the wood upon which we stand. Because Christians are His children, our Father expects us to believe that He, the good and loving Possessor of all things, will provide all that is necessary for our lives. Jesus said, "Or which one of you, if his son asks him for bread, will give him a stone? Or if he asks for a fish, will give him a serpent? If you then, who are evil, know how to give good gifts to your children, how much more will your Father who is in heaven give good things to those who ask him!"[16]

If we are envious of someone's belongings, wealth, or status, it indicates that we are unsure, or do not believe, that the One who, after providing the ultimate sacrifice—Himself—is willing to supply that which has far less value: material provision for His sons and daughters.

Being envious of earthly things is a myopic, worldly understanding of true possessions. Believers in Jesus Christ will someday graciously, freely, inherit and share His created wonders for eternity, true treasure indeed: heavenly, glorious substance that will make all that we have accumulated on the earth be as nothing.

God's Love Is Not Arrogant

Arrogance is the other side of envy's coin. If we are prideful about worldly goods, gifts, or accomplishments, we are boasting that we have provided that which, in truth, God has given freely. We may indeed work hard, but it is God who has given us not only the talents, but the beating hearts and expanding lungs that are necessary

---

15. Deuteronomy 10:14.
16. Matthew 7:9-11.

to accomplish that work, not to mention the air we breathe, the sun that heats the earth, and all the intricate marvels of physics and biology that make this planet livable.

To be condescending toward others consigns us to a status most undesirable and dangerous—opposition to God Himself: "Clothe yourselves, all of you, with humility toward one another, for 'God opposes the proud but gives grace to the humble.'"[17]

Christians must live in the clarity of this truth: We are not the source of our treasures, talents, or position. He is. In the light of the Lord God's unassailable adequacy, we may be conceited about nothing.

God's Love Is Not Rude

The NIV translates this portion of 1 Corinthians 13:5 by stating that God's love "does not dishonor others." Being rude and thus dishonoring others is an understandable furtherance of the effects of pride. We may consider ourselves athletic as we play a game and begin to shout derisively at those who are clumsy and slow, thus putting our victory in jeopardy. We may think we are bright and well-versed, but other "unfortunates" are stupid; so we brush aside those who do not match our acumen. We may think ourselves rich and urbane and look down our noses at those less well-dressed and cultured. If we lift ourselves above others, we live in a hierarchy that exists in our minds but not in the mind of God. This is not the way the God of love thinks or behaves. On the contrary, the King of the universe, the imperium of all knowledge and ability, deliberately placed Himself on the bottom rung of the ladder so we could know and love Him. He loves the ones we rudely dishonor. Mary expressed God's heart when she met Elizabeth and her baby, John, leapt in his mother's womb: "He has shown strength with his arm; he has scattered the proud in the thoughts of their hearts; he has brought down the mighty from their thrones and exalted those

---

17. 1 Peter 5:5b.

of humble estate; he has filled the hungry with good things, and the rich he has sent away empty."[18]

God's Love Is Not Easily Angered

God is lovingly patient, and He is therefore slow to become angry with us when we behave badly. In contrast, rage too often erupts from us when we are not similarly long-suffering with others. We flare up because someone has inconvenienced or disagreed with us. We are often tempted to exact revenge upon those who have disrespected or hurt us. However, the Lord says that such revenge is solely His province, not ours: "Beloved, never avenge yourselves, but leave it to the wrath of God, for it is written, 'Vengeance is mine, I will repay, says the Lord.'"[19] The love of God is not characterized by such anger, which will never produce righteous godliness.[20] We love ourselves too greatly, and our hasty provocations stem from a lack of the maturing of God's self-deprecating love in us. However, He will graciously help us overcome our ill-humor as we ask.

God's Love Does Not Rejoice at Wrongdoing

Christians should not be happy when someone is diminished or shamed due to their sin. Believers in Jesus are spiritual priests[21] and should "deal gently with the ignorant and wayward" because they are, like those disobedient ones, "beset with weakness."[22] Heaven rejoices when a sinner repents.[23] Concerning fellow Christians, we are to restore those who are caught in any transgression, in a spirit of gentleness.[24] Nor should we be secretly pleased when

18. Luke 1:51–53.
19. Romans 12:19.
20. James 1:19–20.
21. 1 Peter 2:4–5.
22. Hebrews 5:2.
23. Luke 15:10.
24. Galatians 6:1.

Christians are afflicted, someone sins against them, or they experience tragedy or misfortune, as if they deserved it. Paul wrote, "If one member suffers, all suffer together; if one member is honored, all rejoice together."[25] Rather, it is God's will that evil is defeated and His loving truth prevails. When we rejoice in wrongdoing done to believer and unbeliever alike, we may self-righteously conclude God is judging them for their sins. Jesus addressed this way of thinking: "There were some present at that very time who told him about the Galileans whose blood Pilate had mingled with their sacrifices. And he answered them, 'Do you think that these Galileans were worse sinners than all the other Galileans, because they suffered in this way? No, I tell you; but unless you repent, you will all likewise perish. Or those eighteen on whom the tower in Siloam fell and killed them: do you think that they were worse offenders than all the others who lived in Jerusalem? No, I tell you; but unless you repent, you will all likewise perish.'"[26]

God the Father loves us and hates evil, which is destructive to the soul. If we are so callous as to rejoice at sinful and destructive offenses, we demonstrate our lack of love for people and for the truth. It is an unbecoming and insidious way for Christians to behave. However, the Lord will forgive us for even this, as we turn and ask for pardon.

Love Bears All, Believes All, Hopes All, Endures All

In this magnificent acclamation of God's love, Paul wrote, "Love bears all things, believes all things, hopes all things, endures all things."[27]

Love suffers but bears up under that agony, by God's strength and grace, and knows resurrection and victory lie ahead. Jesus wept at the tomb of Lazarus. We are not told why. Was He crying

---

25. 1 Corinthians 12:26.
26. Luke 13:1–5.
27. 1 Corinthians 13:7.

over the reality of death and the sadness it brings? Was His weeping an intermingling of profound joy and deep sorrow because He knew in the unfathomable depths of His being that He would die to defeat such death, such soul-crushing grief?[28]

In His love, we endure. We mourn with our brothers and sisters. We weep with those who weep. We link arms and persevere with each other in trial. Love "believes all things"—the truth that the Lord possesses the incomparable power and ability to cause everything to work together for good, for those who love Him.[29] All is well and will be well. We encourage each other in this eternal truth, because all that we presently know will pass away. Love, however, thanks be to our God and Savior, will never end. It will go on and on, forever.

God's Love Never Ends

The love of our God is not weak or wavering. Jeremiah, although mourning over the devastation of his people, wrote two of the most marvelous verses in Scripture:

> The steadfast love of the LORD never ceases;
> his mercies never come to an end;
> they are new every morning;
> great is your faithfulness
> (Lamentations 3:22–23).

As Paul looked toward the conclusion of this elegant symphony of love in Corinthians; indeed, as he looked toward the conclusion of all earthly days, He wrote that spiritual gifts—prophesy, tongues—one day will cease. Knowledge itself will pass away. But not love. Love—not faith, not hope—is the greatest of all.

The love of God is eternal and unrelenting. It will. Never. Stop. The supply of mercy God possesses cannot be exhausted. Your sins cannot overcome it. All of the evil that people have done

---

28. John 11:33–44.
29. Romans 8:28.

or will do cannot overwhelm it. His love conquers every guilt, every shame, every sin, without exception. He will love you as His precious child forever.

Jesus the Servant

If that was not enough—and it is—let us return to this astounding truth: God is our servant. Let us tread carefully here, but we cannot deny the truths He proclaimed. Jesus, our Lord, Creator, and Savior, spoke the following words about Himself: "Stay dressed for action and keep your lamps burning, and be like men who are waiting for their master to come home from the wedding feast, so that they may open the door to him at once when he comes and knocks. Blessed are those servants whom the master finds awake when he comes. Truly, I say to you, he will dress himself for service and have them recline at table, and he will come and serve them."[30]

What kind of God is this? What will you and I do when the glorious God who offered Himself in sacrifice for rebellious sinners like us, stoops to serve us dinner?

Our Humbled Inability

This chapter is brief. We cannot—would be unable to—exalt the totality of His love if we wrote countless volumes during our brief life span. These lyrics from the stirring hymn by Frederick Lehman come to mind:

> Could we with ink the ocean fill,
> And were the skies of parchment made,
> Were every stalk on earth a quill,
> And every man a scribe by trade;
> To write the love of God above
> Would drain the ocean dry;

---

30. Luke 12:35–37.

The God of Love

> Nor could the scroll contain the whole,
> Though stretched from sky to sky.[31]

This chapter is woefully inadequate. Nevertheless, enough is written here about our God to give Him glory forever and ever.

And we will.

He shall be, finally, the God we know.

---

31. Lehman, *The Love of God,* 3rd verse.

Bibliography

Acton, John Emerich Edward Dalberg, Lord Acton to Bishop Mandell Creighton, April 5, 1887. In *Historical Essays and Studies*. Edited by John N. Figgis and Reginald V. Laurence. London: Macmillan, 1907.

Bauer, Walter. *A Greek-English Lexicon of the New Testament and Other Early Christian Literature*. 3rd ed. Revised and edited by Fredrick W. Danker. Translated by William F. Arndt, F. Wilbur Gingrich, and Fredrick W. Danker. Chicago: University of Chicago Press, 2000.

Brannan, Rick, et al. *The Lexham English Septuagint*. Bellingham: Lexham, 2012.

Day, Edward, P. *Day's Collacon: an Encyclopedia of Prose Quotations*. New York: International, 1884.

Leham, Fredrick M. (1917). *The Love of God*. 3rd verse by Nehorai, Meir Benn Issac. 1050. http://library.timelesstruths.org/music/The_Love_of_God/.

Luz, Ulrich. *Matthew 8–20: A Commentary*. Hermeneia. Edited by Helmut Koester. Minneapolis: Augsburg, 2001.

Morris, Leon. *The Gospel According to Matthew*. The Pillar New Testament Commentary. Grand Rapids: Eerdmans, 1992.

Orwell, George. *Animal Farm: A Fairy Story*. 1st ed. London: Secker & Warburg, 1945. http://www.george-orwell.org/Animal_Farm/9.html.

Thomson, Jim. *Deeper: A Call to Discipleship*. Charleston: Amazon, 2011.

Zodhiates, Spiros. *The Complete Word Study Dictionary: New Testament*. Chattanooga: AMG. 2000.

www.ingramcontent.com/pod-product-compliance
Lightning Source LLC
Chambersburg PA
CBHW070919160426
43193CB00011B/1529